"Speaks directly to both leaders and managers about the personal benefits to be realized when leaders learn to manage and managers learn to lead."

M. Anthony Burns, Chairman, President & CEO, Ryder System, Inc.

"Craig Hickman offers unique insight on how both leaders and managers can tap their creative potential to achieve sustained growth and lasting excellence."

Peter E. McNally, Vice President, Brand Marketing, Frito-Lay, Inc.

"A balanced approach to the need to take full advantage of existing skills, whether they be leadership or managerial—a book worth reading. A help to many in understanding strengths and weaknesses."

Kay R. Whitmore, President, Eastman Kodak

"There is great danger in thinking that leaders alone or managers for that matter will save business. Both effective management and leadership are essential. Everyone should read *Mind of a Manager, Soul of a Leader*—it is a blueprint for operating in our global marketplace."

Joseph A. Cannon, Chairman and CEO, Geneva Steel

"Enlightening! After reading so much about the value of leadership, it is often easy to discount the true manager. Craig Hickman has used his experience and a clear, concise writing style to illustrate that good organizations must use both managers and leaders to tap their full potential. *Mind of a Manager, Soul of a Leader* will provide an excellent reference to be used again and again."

Michael L. Eagle, President & CEO, IVAC Corporation

"Open minded 'leaders' and 'managers' alike will greatly improve their management and organizational skills by understanding and employing the insights provided in this book. Craig Hickman presents an enlightened analysis of modern business management."

Richard L. Beattie, President & CEO (Retired), Star Kist Foods, Inc.

"This book contains a fundamental penetrating truth—leaders need managers, managers need leaders. And we all need Hickman's clarity and insight."

Ian Erskine, Lord of Rerrick (U.K.)

"Hickman provides great insight into the necessity and art of blending management and leadership."

John R. Evans, Vice President, First Interstate Bank

"Craig Hickman has compiled a valuable addition to the literature — a most readable examination of leadership and management styles. His book is equally valuable to CEOs, individuals, or human resources professionals charged with identifying talent and taking appropriate development action. At last, a new look at a critical issue for the 1990s!"

Harry E. Gordon, Jr., Director of Executive Resources, Hercules Incorporated

"Craig Hickman has written an easy-to-read, thought-provoking book that clearly sets forth the concept of leadership versus management and provides the reader with specific examples and a framework for personal application."

Thomas P. O'Connor, Senior Vice President, New York Life Insurance Co.

"*Mind of a Manager, Soul of a Leader* is an excellent book of its kind and provides a thought-provoking insight into the art of management and leadership in major organizations. I can highly recommend it."

David Harden, Managing Director, Lockyer, Bradshaw & Wilson Ltd.

"The message of this book is of crucial importance to the future of business in the global economy."

Dilip V. Kulkarni, Chairman & CEO, Systematic Management

"*Mind of a Manager, Soul of a Leader* is the only book on 'leadership' in business to offer hard lessons, not glib overgeneralizations. It frustrates our wish that the conduct of business be self-evident and obvious. It pleases us with stories of how real people fell into the traps of wishful thinking about leadership and how in the nick of time they got out of those traps by doing the hard thinking beyond simple choosing of leadership over management or choosing management over leadership."

Richard Greene, Xerox Corp., Author of Japanese AI Techniques

"It took many years and much pain to believe in my gut what Craig Hickman teaches to the brain. Management in this era of accelerating change is a complex challenge; Craig's book helps to make it simpler."

Peter W. Schutz, Former President & CEO, Porsche AG

"Craig Hickman presents a comprehensive, enlightened work on not only how to understand the basic tension between management and leadership but more importantly, how to capitalize on these tensions and create the blend and mix that will result in long-term superior performance."

Jack Omlor, Chief Financial Officer, Paper Manufacturers Co.

"Hickman does an excellent job in putting forth the art of blending management and leadership. Everything about this book is first-rate—invaluable for both managers and leaders."

Reid A. Robison, Vice President and General Manager, O.C. Tanner

"*Mind of a Manager, Soul of a Leader* proposes an innovative solution to the organizational dilemma between thinkers and doers prevalent in many closely held businesses as well as corporate empires—a realistic answer to many destructive organizational practices apparent in today's business community."

Lawrence W. Tuller, Author of The Battle-Weary Executive

"This book is pragmatic, realistic, and insightful . . . it will serve as a valuable gut-check for every manager seeking to be a winner."

Martin C. Miler, Chairman & President, Hibernia Corporation

"Craig Hickman's premise is profound. It is also enormously significant for the decade of the '90s. The balance and synergy between leadership and management is powerfully and clearly communicated in specific, practical ways. Everyone—parents, educators, professionals, students, etc.—not just business executives, should benefit immediately and ultimately from deeply understanding this 'idea whose time has come'."

Stephen R. Covey, Chairman of the Covey Leadership Center,
Author of The 7 Habits of Highly Effective People

"Hickman provides interesting insight into the natural conflict that exists between the leader and manager, but observes that exceptional companies encourage *both* skill sets."

Ron Dollens, President and CEO, Advanced Cardiovascular Systems, Inc.

"This book breaks with the practice of adopting the latest management hobby-horse to move a company forward. Instead, it plugs the reader into a strategy for using the natural strengths of leaders and managers in every corporation as the power source to increase productivity and profits."

Bruce L. Christensen, President and Chief Executive Officer,
Public Broadcasting Service

"Integrity, ethics, and valuing—these are words necessary in every executive's day-to-day operating philosophy to successfully blend management and leadership. Craig Hickman's new book spells this out in clear and concise terms."

F.G. "Buck" Rodgers, Former Vice President/Marketing, IBM,
Author of The IBM Way

"*Mind of a Manager, Soul of a Leader* picks up where *Creating Excellence* left off and provides an indispensible tool for any executive's kit."

Thomas R. Grimm, Chairman and CEO, PSWW, Inc. (Price Savers)

"Hickman's holistic view, illustrated with his own business and consulting experience, is that a thriving bottom line depends on neither one management style nor the other, but on a winning mix of both."

Wayne Gooding, Editor of Canadian Business

"The conflict between the managers and the leaders within our organization has been an ongoing challenge to overcome. Now, Craig Hickman has presented insight into both of these styles, and has shown that this conflict can, in fact, be positive. This book is required reading for our managers."

Eric R. Despain, President & CEO, Christensen Boyles Corporation

"Craig Hickman has perfected the balance between managing and leading."

Kenneth Blanchard, Ph.D., Coauthor of The One Minute Manager

Mind of a Manager
Soul of a Leader

Craig R. Hickman

WILEY

John Wiley & Sons, Inc.

New York • Chichester • Brisbane • Toronto • Singapore

To my wife, Pamela,
    who generously gives,
    not only love and support,
    but balance.

Copyright © 1990 by Craig R. Hickman

Published by John Wiley & Sons, Inc.
All rights reserved. Published simultaneously in Canada.

Reproduction or translation of any part of this work beyond that permitted by Section 107 or 108 of the 1976 United States Copyright Act without the permission of the copyright owner is unlawful. Requests for permission or further information should be addressed to the Permissions Department, John Wiley & Sons, Inc.

This publication is designed to provide accurate and authoritative information in regard to the subject matter covered. It is sold with the understanding that the publisher is not engaged in rendering legal, accounting, or other professional service. If legal advice or other expert assistance is required, the services of a competent professional person should be sought. *From a Declaration of Principles jointly adopted by a Committee of the American Bar Association and a Committee of Publishers.*

Library of Congress Cataloging-in-Publication Data
Hickman, Craig R.
  Mind of a manager, soul of a leader / Craig R. Hickman.
    p.   cm.
  Includes bibliographical references.
  ISBN 0-471-61715-6
  1. Management.   2. Leadership.   3. Corporate culture.
4. Executive ability. I. Title.
HD31.H4815   1990   89-28494
658.4'09 — dc20   CIP

Printed in the United States of America

90 91 10 9 8 7 6 5 4 3 2 1

Preface

During the 1980s, people and organizations pursued "excellence" with great vigor and determination. And, while creating excellence will probably continue as a mainstay during the 1990s, a new quest has clearly emerged: the pursuit of integration and balance. Individuals, families, organizations, and society in general increasingly see the need for greater harmony among professional careers and personal relationships, worldly success and spiritual fulfillment, economic prosperity and environmental protection, accomplishment and peace of mind, tough-mindedness and gentleness, immediate gratification and enduring joy, this generation and future generations.

In organizations this gravitation toward balance has encouraged business people to begin integrating incremental strategies with innovative breakthroughs, cultural values with corporate policies, stability and security with change and opportunity, flexible processes with structured systems, and short-term gains with long-term progress. The complex global business environment of the 1990s demands that we go much further in this direction. However, given the growing pressures, complexity, change, and competition facing business organizations today, most executives find themselves confronted with an escalating conflict and schism between the managerial and leadership requirements of organizations. An "either/or" mentality dominates at a time when organizations most desperately need the best of both.

When I talk about balancing management and leadership, I do not mean that managers should become more like leaders or that leaders should become more like managers. Quite to the contrary, the new balance needed by organizations today requires the full deployment of both managers and leaders, individually building upon their own unique perspectives and talents, while deeply appreciating those of the other camp. Managers and leaders must harmonize quite strong and different orientations to create the very best organizations of the future. Such balance comes not from within one person, but through the effective, open, and empowered interaction of different people who would otherwise succumb to counterproductive conflict.

Most books proceed in a straight line from page one to the end. However, I have intentionally written this book for rapid random access. When you scan the chapter titles, you may find your curiosity piqued by Chapter 6, Strategy Plus Culture, or you may want to look first at Chapter 28, Complexity Plus Simplicity. Fine. I would recommend you read the Introduction first, then start anywhere you'd like and skip around at will. I might suggest that if, after reading the Introduction, you consider yourself more oriented toward the managerial mind, you will probably appreciate the realism and practicality of the chapters in Sections II through IV. You might begin with chapters in these sections and then come back to Section I later. On the other hand, if you find yourself leaning toward the soul of leadership, you might begin with the chapters in Section I, which provide a conceptual framework that informs the later chapters.

I have organized and grouped chapters around five major organizational success factors, but you shouldn't feel constrained to read a whole section before moving to another. Browse freely, reading whichever chapter catches your interest or addresses an issue with which you are currently wrestling. Each chapter addresses a potential conflict or schism between the managerial and leadership orientations, and then it looks at the unique ways in which blending and balancing the two can create more than the sum of the parts.

After you read a chapter, however, I suggest that you do three things. First, think of at least three situations in your own experience where you have observed or displayed one or both of the orientations described in the chapter. Second, roughly rate yourself as more of a manager or more of a leader with respect to the issue in question. You may be surprised to find that sometimes you manage, sometimes you lead, and sometimes you do a bit of both. In fact, as you read each chapter, keep in mind that most people operate with a combination of managerial and leadership skills. Rarely does one individual always manager or always lead. Third, think about your organization in terms of the issue presented in the chapter. Is your organization management-dominated, leadership-driven, conflict-oriented, vacillation-prone, or balanced and integrated?

You also might use this book in a management team setting, where you read and discuss one or more of the chapters as a group. Can you identify the managers in your group? The leaders? Do you value each other's viewpoints? Do your viewpoints harmonize or conflict? Does your team tap the natural tension between management and leadership? Should you bolster one or the other? Should you find better ways to integrate the two in certain situations? In the case of Section I, discuss what kind of management/leadership environment exists in your organization and what you might do to make it more balanced and integrated. This kind of organizational mind and soul searching can stimulate team building, open up communications, and help your organization benefit from more effective orchestration of strategy, culture, change, effectiveness, and results. It also can put you on the path to creating a world-class organization.

Tension always exists between managers and leaders. It's a natural phenomenon. If tapped successfully, it can fulfill the promise of "one plus one equals three." As you read a chapter, don't ask "Which works better?" Rather ask, "What combination works best?" Only by clearly understanding the value and importance of differing perspectives can you find the right mixture, the right blend, the right integration for the unique needs and circumstances of your own organization.

Finally, have fun with this book. Gaining new insights into yourself, your associates, and your organization can be exhilarating, surprising, uplifting, even embarrassing. At times, most managers and leaders take themselves too seriously, so lighten up. I sincerely hope you will find this book enjoyable as well as informative. If you encounter a situation you would like to discuss, come up with a question you'd like to ask, want to offer a different perspective, or just want to argue a point, call me at 1-800-537-3065. I'll foot the bill.

Craig R. Hickman

Acknowledgments

I owe acknowledgments to several people for their contributions to this book. First, Michael Snell performed the invaluable role of helping me develop, write, and edit this book. I cannot thank him enough for his unique contribution. His perspectives and talents bring an appropriate balance to our collaborations. I also want to thank my business partner, Les Forslund, for his enduring commitment to helping people in organizations constantly grow and for sharing with me his insightful and patient advice during this book project. Other associates at Management Perspectives Group provided crucial contributions. Eric Marchant helped create and write the conclusion and appendices to this book and offered numerous useful critiques and suggestions. Craig Russell provided the development of Appendix C. Debi Smith provided administrative support during the final stages of this effort. Mary Kowalczyk and her company, Word Masters, performed amazingly, as usual, typing and proofing the manuscript through its several drafts.

I would also like to thank Dilip Kulkarni, Chairman and CEO of Systematic Management Services, the parent firm of Management Perspectives Group, for his patience, wisdom, and encouragement during this effort. He, along with key associates Bill Drake, Stan Sellars, and Foster Acton, provide another source of balance to me personally and to Management Perspectives Group. Also, Ken Shelton and his firm, Executive Excellence, have made important contributions toward this book's publication.

Many, many thanks go to my publisher, John Wiley & Sons, for remaining solid and professional in a sea of industry changes. Particularly, I want to thank Senior Editor John Mahaney for his careful and constant nurturing of the project from the beginning, and to Gwyneth Jones, Publisher, for her enthusiasm and perceptiveness along the way.

My wife and family continue to support me with understanding in all my endeavors and particularly during the "crunches." Members of my extended family and many close friends also deserve thanks for their ongoing interest and contribution to my writing efforts. In particular, I want to thank my father, Winston Hickman, for his valuable comments on the manuscript.

Finally, I must thank the many people and organizations with whom I have worked as a management consultant over the years because they have taught me much about management and leadership. I am deeply indebted and grateful to those who have inspired the many chapters of this book for the experiences we shared. Their struggles, their victories, and even their temporary setbacks have greatly influenced me in my quest to help, in some small way, the men and women who manage and lead today's organizations.

Contents

Introduction: Tapping the Natural Tension Between Managers and Leaders

Why Quality, Service, Innovation, Cost, and All the Other Popular Routes to Competitive Advantage Are Not Enough

Today the best business managers and leaders are engaged in a feverish search for that often-elusive advantage that will propel them and their organizations to greater success. This anxious quest has produced great benefits for our organizations, because many searchers have found advantages, such as some new approach to enhancing product quality, strengthening customer service, stimulating innovations, or reducing costs, that work some magic—for a time. When this happens, others jump on the bandwagon. It seldom takes long for the advantage to lose some of its magic. Then everyone starts looking for another advantage, and then another, and then still another—until the search becomes a sort of möbius strip, the one-sided mathematical paradox that gives you a sense of forward progress but forever returns you to the point where you began.

Rubbermaid, Marriott, Merck, and Emerson, among other organizations, have been pursuing courses that represent some of the more popular current routes to success, but where, in the long run, will these routes take them? Will such routes remain productive forever? Maybe. But maybe not.

Rubbermaid points to its quality products, developed through one of the best total quality environments in the country; Marriott touts its unbeatable customer service through its unwavering attention to service details; Merck prides itself on its ability to continually develop new products with state-of-the-art R&D management; and Emerson Electric heralds its talent for cutting, minimizing, and holding costs while still producing viable products. Others hope the secret lies in advanced technology, marketing creativity, speed to market, downsizing, white-collar productivity, decentralization, or total employee involvement.

While companies riding on the various bandwagons have gained some degree of short-term competitive advantage, the complexity of the global marketplace renders doing one or two things very well — or even best — not enough for survival, much less lasting success. In the future, sustained advantage and enduring results will hinge on the ability of management to rise above the noise and commotion of the parade and grasp the simple, universal principles that tie all the success secrets together. In this regard, businesspeople might do well to mimic physicists, who constantly seek to unite all the fundamental principles of matter and energy into one grand unified theory.

In this book I offer a candidate for the grand unified theory of business management: Enduring results and the ultimate competitive advantage come from tapping the natural tension between managers and leaders. As described in more detail later in this introduction and throughout the rest of the book, managers tend to be more practical, reasonable, and decisive, while leaders tend to be more visionary, empathetic, and flexible. Tapping the natural tension between managers and leaders allows executives and organizations to use quality, service, technology, cost control, innovation, marketing creativity, speed to market, and every other success variable not as myopic fads or isolated factors, but as appropriate and timely aspects of a dynamic management/leadership environment. When this happens, the resulting balanced, integrated organization can turn in superior performance year after year after year.

One of the most alarming current fads holds that leaders make much more of a difference than managers when it comes to guiding organizations to competitive advantage and enduring results. This wrongheaded notion has given too many people a distorted picture of managers as dull, impersonal, plodding, tedious, unimaginative, and stagnant souls. Of course, everyone would rather be a leader, because leaders, as we've been told, are inspiring, personable, charismatic, creative, and visionary folks. And indeed, managers do differ from leaders, and a natural tension does arise between the typical managerial and leadership orientations. But the real secret to long-term, enduring success lies not in turning the tension into conflict or in trying to make the tension go away, but in accepting and encouraging the differences in order to tap the power of the tension. In the old television westerns, viewers could tell the "good guys" from the "bad guys" by the color of their hats. Saddled with a similarly superficial good guy/bad guy distinction, some managers try to duck the label and masquerade as leaders by simply donning the white hats or they attempt to undermine leaders by shooting holes in their leadership images. By the same token, some leaders, feeling smug and self-satisfied, look benevolently down on the mortal world of day-to-day management from their high horses treating managers as necessary evils, or patronizing them with a few words of encouragement. Both act as if a showdown will erupt at sunup and whoever emerges the least wounded will win.

This adversarial perspective, so unconsciously dominant in business thinking today, has fostered organizational environments where managers too often stifle leaders and leaders too often ignore managers. Thus a growing schism between the two orientations has created a genuine threat, as well as an incredible opportunity. The opportunity will be seized by smart management teams which tune out the good guy/bad guy view in favor of one where leaders genuinely value the abilities and roles of managers and *vice versa*. The best executives know that their organizations need both.

Early in my business career I worked closely with Tom Mullaney and Phil Matthews, then president and executive vice-president, respectively, of Dart Industries, a $2 billion diversified firm at the time with over 100 divisions, including Tupperware, Westbend Appliances,

Wilsonart, Duracell Batteries, Thatcher Glass, Miracle Maid, and other chemical, plastics, and consumer products businesses. Their combined impact and influence on me was, I'm sure, much greater than either one of them realized at the time. Tom Mullaney had been a partner at McKinsey & Company before moving to PepsiCo and running the Wilson Sporting Goods Division. Phil Matthews had been a financial and operating executive with Frito-Lay, also part of PepsiCo. Through their insightful management and leadership, I was immersed in both the McKinsey way of thinking and the PepsiCo way of operating. At Dart Industries, the two men strove to create a truly great corporation which, I believe, they would have accomplished if Justin Dart, chairman and CEO of Dart Industries, had not set his heart on merging his company with Kraft Foods. What I came to appreciate most about these two executives was their comprehensive outlook when it came to performance. They seemed to understand intuitively and analytically the need to regulate the tension between management and leadership in order to bring about organizational greatness. It wasn't enough to attain a competitive advantage based on quality, service, or any other particular organizational characteristic. No, enduring competitive advantage came less from any one thing or few things you did than from the overall way you managed the enterprise.

While working closely with these two executives, I grew to appreciate the ways in which they could tap the natural tension between their managers and leaders. They even knew how to tap Justin Dart's entrepreneurial drive and keep it alive within Dart Industries. Unfortunately, Dart himself, who did not share their talents at emphasizing a balanced, integrated organization, allowed his entrepreneurial leadership to overshadow the rest of what was going on within the company by pushing through the Dart-Kraft merger. The merger may have launched the tenth largest corporation in America at the time, but it also marked the beginning of a disaster. Tom Mullaney resigned, and Phil Matthews, who became chief financial officer of Dart & Kraft, resigned a short time later. A few years after that, Dart & Kraft undid the merger and sold off the pieces of the company. The once-vibrant dream of creating a world-class corporation at Dart Industries had died. Fortunately, however, the same dream survives in a growing number of other organizations around the world today.

PepsiCo is one of them. PepsiCo's former chairman, Donald Kendall, once described PepsiCo as the "ultimate capitalistic engine." Whether it can honestly lay claim to this distinction or not, PepsiCo certainly does produce some of the most sought after executives in America and the world today. Why? Because PepsiCo has discovered, like Mullaney and Matthews, that the ultimate competitive advantage lies not in controlling one or several success variables, but in tapping the natural tension between management and leadership to balance and integrate all the success variables into one dynamic whole.

PepsiCo's CEO, Wayne Calloway, knowing that his organization's success hinges equally on the minds of his managers and the souls of his leaders, spends so much of his time talking about and working toward the development of both in his organization that his thinking has spread far beyond his own direct reporting relationships. Throughout the organization, managers strive to nurture leaders as well as other managers, and leaders strive to develop managers as well as other leaders. As Calloway says, "We take eagles and teach them to fly in formation." As a result, this organization enjoys the best that both management and leadership can offer. Leaders spread their wings to soar and create, while managers spread their wings to exploit all the success that vision and creativity make possible. In fact, the balance and integration among management and leadership orientations at PepsiCo may be unsurpassed.

Not only do executives take performance evaluations of their subordinates seriously, but subordinates treat their own evaluations of executives as if the very life of the organization depended on them. PepsiCo people are given broad experience throughout the company and a lot of responsibility at an early age. One of these, Peter McNally, with whom I have worked, was directing a $500 million snack-food business at age twenty-four. Peter exemplifies the strong leader who appreciates the importance of management, and he is committed to the balanced and integrated approach that distinguishes PepsiCo's management/leadership environment.

At the company's core lies a deep devotion to developing people and balancing the need for managerial constancy with the need for leadership vision. To be sure, some of PepsiCo's fast-track units make others look like they are standing still, but this simply underscores the fact that some units require aggressive leadership while others require steady management. Interestingly, this company achieves both by tailoring the unique talents and capabilities of every manager and leader to specific and different situations within the organization. Every manager and leader follows an individualized development track that receives a great deal of scrutiny to make sure that he or she is progressing smoothly. Those who can't "cut the mustard" find jobs quite easily outside the company, because so many other organizations admire PepsiCo's management and leadership development process.

Tension naturally and constantly arises throughout the organization between the different orientations of the managers and leaders, but the company harnesses this tension to drive a dynamo of productivity that innovates new products, markets with imagination, operates consistently, and strategically outsmarts its competitors. Perhaps PepsiCo has become the ultimate capitalistic engine.

In this book, you will read about a variety of situations in which managers and leaders might well reach for their six-shooters if they do not value each other's skills and orientations. By exploring the sometimes obvious and often subtle differences between managers and leaders, I hope you can gain a deeper appreciation of each. This deeper understanding should help you to better determine when, how, and why different doses of management and leadership make sense in different situations. By so doing, you can begin creating the ultimate capitalistic engine. However, before I share with you some of the lessons I've learned while trying to figure out how to build such an engine myself, I'd like to draw a brief sketch of what I call the manager's mind and the leader's soul. I also want to review the historical and current thinking about managers and leaders that has brought us to what I think is a vital turning point for people in organizations today.

Managers' Minds and Leaders' Souls

The words "manager" and "leader" are metaphors representing two opposite ends of a continuum. "Manager" tends to signify the more analytical, structured, controlled, deliberate, and orderly end of the continuum, while "leader" tends to occupy the more experimental, visionary, flexible, uncontrolled, and creative end. Given these fairly universal metaphors of contrasting organizational behavior, I like to think of the prototypical manager as the person who brings the thoughts of the mind to bear on daily organizational problems. In contrast, the leader brings the feelings of the soul to bear on those same problems. Certainly, managers and leaders both have minds and souls, but they each tend to emphasize one over the other as they function in organizations. The mind represents the analytical, calculating, structuring, and ordering side of tasks and organizations. The soul, on the other hand, represents the visionary, passionate, creative, and flexible side.

Both managers and leaders have attained success in the past, and they will go on doing so. Former famous CEOs with managers' minds abound: Harold Geneen of ITT and Henry Ford, II, of Ford Motor Company. So do those with leaders' souls: Ray Kroc of McDonald's and Walt Disney of the Walt Disney Company. Today you can see plenty of manager-type CEOs: John Akers of IBM, Roger Smith of General Motors, and Charles Knight of Emerson Electric. And you can find just as many leader types: Ross Perot, founder of EDS and Perot Systems; Ted Turner of Turner Broadcasting; and Steven Jobs of Apple Computer fame, now at the helm of NeXT. In the realm of sports, head football coaches have guided their teams to Super Bowl wins both by managing and leading. Tom Landry of the Dallas Cowboys was a consumate manager, while John Madden of the then Oakland Raiders represented the committed leader.

Just how do the manager's mind and the leader's soul approach all the issues that confront an organization? What follows is a summary of some of the more important differences between managerial and leadership orientations. As you consider these differences, think about your own orientations and how you compare with the people around you. You may find yourself feeling and acting like a manager compared to one person and like a leader compared to another. This simply points out that a person at a given point on a continuum between management and leadership will find some people more management oriented and others more leadership oriented by comparison. Keep in mind that most people do not find themselves at either extreme of a management-leadership continuum; rather they possess some combination of management and leadership orientations with an overall preference for one or the other.

The five sets of manager-leader continuums displayed in the next few pages present the differences between managers and leaders that you'll find exemplified and discussed in chapters six through forty-nine.

		Management-Oriented	Leadership-Oriented	
Competitive Strategy/ Advantage	Strategy	●—●—●—●—●—●—●—●		Culture
	Danger	●—●—●—●—●—●—●—●		Opportunity
	Version	●—●—●—●—●—●—●—●		Vision
	Isolate	●—●—●—●—●—●—●—●		Correlate
	Solutions	●—●—●—●—●—●—●—●		Problems
	Markets	●—●—●—●—●—●—●—●		Customers
	Rivals	●—●—●—●—●—●—●—●		Partners
	Incremental	●—●—●—●—●—●—●—●		Sweeping
	Weaknesses	●—●—●—●—●—●—●—●		Strengths

First, in terms of competitive strategy and advantage, the manager's mind tends to preoccupy itself with strategic thinking and strategy formulation, while the leader's soul tends to gravitate toward strategy implementation and culture building. The difference boils down to analytical positioning in the marketplace versus sensitivity in applying an organization's culture to the marketplace.

The manager's mind also remains alert to the dangers or the failure-prevention side of strategy, while the leader's soul stays attuned to the opportunities or the success-enhancement side. When it comes to thinking about the future, the leader's soul delights in comprehensive, global, and long-term visions, while the manager's mind drifts more naturally toward specific and concrete versions of what might happen tomorrow. When addressing strategic issues, the manager's mind zeros in on and isolates variables and particular components in order to address them and resolve them, while the leader's soul tends to embrace a larger, more holistic picture that correlates one issue with another in order to sense and feel the implications for the organization as a whole.

The manager's mind worries about the business problems that can threaten the company's strategic or competitive advantage in the marketplace and constantly looks for specific and immediate solutions. The leader's soul, on the other hand, welcomes problems and even goes looking for them because problems keep the organization on its toes. In the case of the marketplace, managers tend to look at it in terms of market segments and niches, while leaders tend to think of it in terms of flesh and blood customers buying products and services. And as far as competitive positioning goes, managers concentrate on the individual rivals in the marketplace, the competitors battling for market share and position, while leaders tend to step back and evaluate the overall competitive environment, the entire industry, and the potential for alliances with rivals.

The mind of a manager prefers incremental strategic gains while the soul of a leader embraces sweeping, dramatic strategies. The manager's mind latches onto weaknesses and how to overcome them, the leader's soul gravitates toward strengths and how to build on them.

		Management-Oriented	Leadership-Oriented
Organizational Culture/ Capability	Authority	●—●—●—●—●—●—●—●	Influence
	Uniformity	●—●—●—●—●—●—●—●	Unity
	Programs	●—●—●—●—●—●—●—●	People
	Policy	●—●—●—●—●—●—●—●	Example
	Instruction	●—●—●—●—●—●—●—●	Inspiration
	MBO	●—●—●—●—●—●—●—●	MBWA
	Control	●—●—●—●—●—●—●—●	Empower
	Releasing	●—●—●—●—●—●—●—●	Keeping
	Consistency	●—●—●—●—●—●—●—●	Commitment

In the areas of organizational culture and capability, the manager's mind adheres to the authority structure and hierarchy as the primary means for getting things done within the organization, while the leader's soul worries more about the influence that the leader can bring to bear in shaping the direction, priorities, and emphasis of the organization. In rallying the troops behind a common purpose, the manager's mind generally directs itself to the uniformity of practice needed to get everyone pulling in the same direction; the leader's soul drives more toward unity of purpose without regard to uniformity of practice. The manager's mind relates to programs that will help people develop the attitudes and behaviors necessary to get things done, while the leader's soul relates to people directly and emphasizes individual development over program implementation.

When it comes to directing people and helping them move in the right direction, the manager thinks primarily in terms of policies that will specify and clarify appropriate actions. The leader, however, prefers to exhibit the appropriate behavior he or she wishes others to emulate. Every organization needs skills, and the manager's mind immediately moves toward some kind of instructional curriculum or packaged course that will teach people the right skills. On the other hand, the leader believes deep in his or her soul that people will rise to challenges and self-develop the right skills if they feel inspired to strive to the utmost of their potential.

Every organization also requires objectives and the assignment of individuals and departments to tasks that will achieve those goals. Here, the manager's mind loves the management-by-objectives (MBO) approach. The leader, however, would much rather practice management by walking around (MBWA), talking with people, getting in touch with their roles within the organization, and learning how they perceive their roles, all in a very informal, unstructured manner. Managers like control; leaders prefer empowerment. With people joining and leaving the organization on a regular basis, the manager's mind characteristically focuses on the reprimanding and terminating side when people don't do their jobs, while the leader's soul concerns itself more with developing and keeping people even when they turn in less than sterling performances. Consistency occupies the manager's mind; commitment engages the leader's soul.

		Management- Oriented	Leadership- Oriented	
External/	Stability	●——●——●——●——●——●——●——●		Crisis
Internal	Duplicate	●——●——●——●——●——●——●——●		Originate
Change	Fasten	●——●——●——●——●——●——●——●		Unfasten
	Compromise	●——●——●——●——●——●——●——●		Polarize
	Complexity	●——●——●——●——●——●——●——●		Simplicity
	Reaction	●——●——●——●——●——●——●——●		Proaction
	Plans	●——●——●——●——●——●——●——●		Experiments
	Reorganize	●——●——●——●——●——●——●——●		Rethink
	Refine	●——●——●——●——●——●——●——●		Revolutionize

Change, both external and internal, also has become a way of corporate life. While the manager naturally desires stability, the leader recognizes that crisis can stimulate improvement. Managers try to duplicate the successful efforts of others, but leaders would rather break new ground. Managers fasten, fix, and put things in place as permanent fixtures of the organization. Leaders continually move about the organization, unfastening, unfixing, and removing things to make sure that the organization does not stagnate. When it comes to decision making, managers hammer out compromises, while leaders don't mind polarizing people around extremes to clarify the differences between them. If changes that occur in the external environment often cause a manager's mind to focus on how to react and respond, they stimulate a leader's soul to become proactive, anticipating and even creating change. "Plan for change," argues the manager. "Experiment with it," insists the leader. In this age of rampant reorganization and restructuring, the manager's mind seems to deal with it all very easily. The leader, however, wants to rethink the fundamentals and not be fooled by a reorganization that may not correct real problems. Managers refine existing structures; leaders promote complete revolution.

In the realm of individual style and effectiveness, the manager's mind focuses on methods, while the leader's soul zeros in on motives. Managers are logical thinkers; leaders are lateral thinkers. In other words, the sequential, step-by-step thinking of the manager differs markedly from the nonsequential, unorthodox thinking of the leader. To determine worth, relevance, and contribution,

		Management-Oriented		Leadership-Oriented	
Individual Effectiveness/ Style	Methods	●—●—●—●—●—●—●—●			Motives
	Logical thinking	●—●—●—●—●—●—●—●			Lateral thinking
	Hierarchy	●—●—●—●—●—●—●—●			Equality
	Skepticism	●—●—●—●—●—●—●—●			Optimism
	Smoothing	●—●—●—●—●—●—●—●			Confronting
	Taking charge	●—●—●—●—●—●—●—●			Letting go
	Formality	●—●—●—●—●—●—●—●			Informality
	Science	●—●—●—●—●—●—●—●			Art
	Duties	●—●—●—●—●—●—●—●			Dreams

managers tend to think in terms of hierarchies, while leaders think much more in terms of equality throughout the organization. The manager maintains a skeptical mind, the leader feels tremendous optimism about everything the organization undertakes.

When it comes to conflict, the manager's mind moves to smooth over the conflict, while the leader's soul finds it difficult to avoid confronting conflict. Managers take charge, leaders let go. Managers stress formality; leaders encourage informality. For the manager, it's all a matter of science; for the leader, it's all a matter of art. "Give me duties to perform," says the manager. "Give me dreams to follow," cries the leader.

		Management-Oriented		Leadership-Oriented	
Bottom-Line Performance/ Results	Performance	●—●—●—●—●—●—●—●			Potential
	Dependence	●—●—●—●—●—●—●—●			Independence
	Compensation	●—●—●—●—●—●—●—●			Satisfaction
	Conserving	●—●—●—●—●—●—●—●			Risking
	Tangible	●—●—●—●—●—●—●—●			Intangible
	Present	●—●—●—●—●—●—●—●			Future
	Short-term	●—●—●—●—●—●—●—●			Long-term
	Good	●—●—●—●—●—●—●—●			Better

And we can't forget the bottom line. The manager's mind measures performance, while the leader's soul values the potential of people and organizations to do more than they have in the past.

In the end, the manager tends to create dependence as a final result; the leader, independence. The manager's mind emphasizes compensating people and organizations for the results they get, while the leader's soul knows that satisfaction means more than money. "Let's conserve our resources, assets, and positions," urges the manager. "Let's risk them," shouts the leader. The manager wants tangible results; the leader seeks intangible results. One lives in the present; the other resides in the future. One thinks short-term, the other, long-term. Managers desire good performance; leaders desire better performance.

You may have noticed the word "plus" in this book's table of contents. I want to emphasize it here because I feel strongly that we must replace "either/or" thinking with "plus" thinking. When it comes to lasting superior performance, managers don't have all the answers; neither do leaders. And it's not a matter of simple arithmetic, whereby we add one to the other to get excellence. No, it's a more dynamic equation than that.

One Plus One Equals Three

Most current thinking seems to suggest that all managers should become more leadership oriented. I disagree. I believe managers should not be required to become more like leaders, nor should leaders be required to become more like managers. Rather, both should come to value and emphasize the unique strengths of each other in order to tap the natural tension between them to produce a "one plus one equals three" outcome. This requires blending strong management and strong leadership into one integrated whole where the strengths of leaders combine with, rather than clash with, the strengths of managers, thereby minimizing the weaknesses of both. Managers or leaders who have achieved some of this balance and integration have guided their organizations to greater heights. For example, such CEOs as John Young of Hewlett-Packard, Donald Peterson of Ford, Michael Eisner of Walt Disney, John Sculley of

Apple Computer, Katharine Graham of *The Washington Post*, and husband and wife team Elisabeth Claiborne and Arthur Ortenberg of Liz Claiborne have been able to accomplish more than most CEOs by integrating management and leadership rather than favoring one over the other or pitting one against the other. In the case of John Sculley, many predicted a leadership to management shift when he took over the reigns at Apple Computer from Steven Jobs. On the contrary, Sculley skillfully orchestrated an integration of management and leadership at Apple that continues to deliver world class performance. Of course, none of these CEOs stands as a perfect example, but each has guided his or her organization to greater heights. They achieved this not because they, themselves, became perfect blends of management and leadership, but because they guided their management teams and organizations toward such a blend and balance.

At the dawning of the modern age of management earlier in this century, thinkers such as Frederick Taylor and Max Weber stated that charismatic leaders get organizations started and then pass the baton to the bureaucrats or professional, scientific managers who can run them. However, it wasn't until after World War II, when organizations began getting bigger and more complex, that differences in management philosophy or approach became a serious subject of academic research and executive concern. In the late 1950s, Douglas McGregor was one of the first widely read authors to identify such differences with his Theory X and Theory Y definitions of management, as outlined in his influential book, *The Human Side of Enterprise*. In McGregor's view, the Theory X manager views workers as lazy, unmotivated avoiders of responsibility who crave security and who respond to the coercing, control, and threats of managers. The Theory Y manager, on the other hand, views workers as industrious, motivated takers of responsibility who can actualize themselves and who respond more to encouragement, guidance, and respect.

Years later, in the mid-1970s, Abraham Zaleznik of the Harvard Business School wrote a now-famous article in the *Harvard Business Review* entitled, "Managers and Leaders: Are They Different?" This article captured the interest of managers and leaders everywhere and a decade later led to publication of Zaleznik's book *The Managerial Mystique*, in which he argues that managers exhibit passive and impersonal attitudes toward goals. Managers are compromisers, conservators, regulators, and controllers who gain their self-worth and identity by perpetuating existing systems and organizations. In contrast, leaders display personal and active attitudes toward goals. They are innovators, riskers, and motivators who gain their self-worth and identity by changing and improving existing systems and organizations. While many businesspeople felt that Zaleznik overstated the differences between managers and leaders, his work did cause people to start thinking about the dichotomy.

During this same period of time, James MacGregor Burns, the Pulitzer Prize–winning author and political historian, completed his influential book *Leadership*, in which he distinguished between transformational leaders, who change courses of action and events, and transactional leaders, who make existing courses of action work better. This touched off a research and writing movement, epitomized by Noel Tichy, University of Michigan professor and co-author of *Transformational Leadership*, that is continuing to examine transformation and leadership in organizations.

Another professor at the Harvard Business School, John Kotter, author of *The Leadership Factor*, described the differences between what he called visionary and nonvisionary executives. While a non-visionary executive solves daily problems, meets formally with sub-ordinates, maintains an aloof, rational image, pays attention to weaknesses, and talks about current business activities, a visionary one articulates philosophy, makes informal contact with employees at all levels, projects a receptive, supportive image, pays attention to strengths, and talks about future business goals.

Into this climate came Warren Bennis, a professor of management at USC, who had studied the characteristics of outstanding CEOs and other leaders for his books *Leaders* and *On Becoming A Leader*. Bennis suggested that managers control contracts or exchanges relating to jobs, security, and money and thus produce compliance or spiteful obedience at best. Leaders, on the other hand, invent themselves and in the process empower people and ideas, creating organizational cultures in which people gain a sense of meaning, purpose, and challenge from their work. Bennis popularized the notion that "managers do things right, and leaders do the right thing."

Culminating almost half a century of intense management thought, research, and experience, writers and thinkers in the late 1980s produced a host of books and articles calling for more leadership and less management. *Fortune, Business Week,* and *Forbes* carried cover stories on America's leadership crisis and the need for corporate executives to embrace the new keys to excellence. They trumpeted such traits as trust, vision, participative management, culture building, risk, and commitment. Admired CEOs such as Jack Welch of General Electric began insisting that American enterprise will need leaders, not managers, in order to compete in the wildly changing 1990s. This advice underscored the transfer of academic management and leadership theory to actual executive practice, and it led to the inevitable conclusion that executives can best solve the management/leadership equation by subtracting from one and adding to the other.

Amid all this leadership zeal, only a few voices warned of the danger of overemphasizing leadership at the expense of management. Even Warren Bennis, a strong proponent of leadership, has shaken his head over today's strange worshipping of leaders. *Fortune* Assistant Managing Editor Walter Kiechel, III, as if trying to position the magazine *vis-à-vis* a possible leadership backlash, wrote in his regular column an article entitled, "The Case Against Leaders." In this article, Kiechel fired some shots at leaders:

- Leaders really make far less of a difference than we think.
- Leaders are only as good as the situations in which they find themselves.
- Leaders manipulate people.
- Unchecked, leaders can run off the tracks, taking their organizations with them.
- Leaders do not inspire so-called baby boomers.
- As management becomes more participatory, leaders become increasingly unnecessary.

Kiechel hasn't been singing in the wilderness. Charles Ferguson, a research associate at MIT, who authored a controversial article published in the *Harvard Business Review* entitled, "From the People

Who Brought You Voodoo Economics," argues that the trend toward smaller, entrepreneurial, specialized companies where leaders thrive and managers are disdained may cause great harm to the
United States. From Ferguson's point of view, the "voodoo" competitive doctrine, namely, that only entrepreneurial competitors
can win in the long run, does not ring true. America's true competitiveness and future business strength will only come from large,
well-managed corporations with the incentives and resources to
make a long-term investment in sustained advantage. Of course,
not everyone agrees with this analysis. George Gilder, author of *The
Spirit of Enterprise* and *Microcosm*, and Tom Peters, co-author of *In
Search of Excellence* and author of *Thriving on Chaos*, for example,
argue that America's problems have come about precisely as a result
of large, bureaucratic, stifling, unresponsive organizations.

Ted Levitt, the editor of the *Harvard Business Review*, proposed
in recent letters from the editor that the world needs *all* sizes of
organizations and that no one size or type outshines another. He
also urged managers in large, professionally managed corporations
to take great care not to let routines and rational decision-making
processes keep them from staying in "solid contact with the things
about which decisions must be made." In essence, Levitt is calling
for the effective managing of the natural tension between managers
and leaders, urging managers to not get wrapped up in bureaucratic
red tape and leaders to value the role of effective systems, structure,
and size. I applaud Levitt for adding his tempering and seasoned
voice to the debate.

Another veteran observer, Peter Drucker, author of *The New
Realities* and many other management books, has tried to convince
us "that management is, above all else, a very few, essential principles." These principles, according to Drucker, govern what managers and leaders do best. In reality, Drucker suggests we need to
integrate all the principles of management and leadership, blending both innovation and stability, both order and flexibility. This
sort of thinking provides an enlightened solution to the manage-
ment/leadership equation: We need to add one to the other with
careful blending.

I agree with those who express a generous and more synthe-
sizing attitude toward managers and leaders, those who think in
terms of "combined with" rather than "either/or." We need it all:
stability plus agility, large plus small, unchanging plus changing,
constancy plus creativity, broad plus narrow, control plus empowerment, technology plus people, practicality plus integrity. In short,
we need management *plus* leadership. This does not mean that we
can simply or easily blend the two orientations or somehow engineer a graceful balancing act. Some situations, such as a business-
threatening financial crisis, demand a heavy dose of management.
Others, such as a repositioning for the emergence of a united European Economic Community, require a strong measure of leadership. Most require some degree of both, the particular mixture vary-
ing just as much as do the situations in which leaders and managers
find themselves.

A natural tension has always existed between managers and
leaders: Managers seek stability, while leaders thrive in crisis; managers exercise authority, while leaders leverage their influence;
managers duplicate, while leaders originate; managers instruct,
while leaders inspire. Tension. It can exist within a single individual, within an organizational unit, within a company, within a strategic alliance of companies, in governments, and among allied
countries. Left to build into animosity, such tension usually leads to
failure, mismanagement, or marginal performance. However, committed people can harness this tension to generate unprecedented
levels of competitive advantage, organizational effectiveness, and
human fulfillment that put the old "one plus one equals two" approach to shame. One plus one, it turns out, *can* equal three.

By highlighting the natural tension between management and
leadership in this book's many short chapters, I hope to show you
something about tapping this tension. Once you know how to do
this in different situations, you should be able to create an empowered
management/leadership environment that can exploit change, master
complexity, maintain competitive advantage over the long term,
and achieve lasting excellence in a world of global competition.

I

Management/ Leadership Environments

The best of both management and leadership fuels the ultimate capitalistic engine and all world-class performers. To obtain the best of both, you need to understand not only their respective attributes but the many small and large differences between them. And you must match just the right mixture of them to your situation or environment. In an effort to help you reach both these goals, I have developed a management/leadership matrix that shows how different types of management/leadership environments generally approach five major success factors for the 1990s. You should take a look at the matrix on the next page before reading the first five chapters, each of which spotlights one of the basic types of management/leadership environments.

For each of the basic types of management/leadership environments, I provide in the following five chapters concrete examples of

The Management/Leadership Matrix

	Types of Management/Leadership Environments				
Success Factors	*Management-Dominated*	*Leadership-Driven*	*Conflict-Oriented*	*Vacillation-Prone*	*Balanced and Integrated*
Competitive strategy/ advantage	Pursue same-game strategies	Formulate new-game strategies	Develop both same- and new-game strategies	Follow reactive strategies	Implement changing-game strategies
Organizational culture/ capability	Perpetuate cultures	Create cultures	Change and provoke cultures	Confuse cultures	Renew cultures
External/ internal change	Strive for stability	Thrive on crisis	Force stability and crisis together	Shift between stability and crisis	Blend stability and crisis
Individual effectiveness/ style	Prefer a structured approach	Favor an unstructured approach	Choose a loose, tight approach	Exhibit an uncertain approach	Promote a dynamic approach
Bottom-line performance/ results	Focus on tangible short-term results	Seek for intangible long-term results	Want both tangible short-term and intangible long-term results	Obtain marginal or negative results	Balance tangible short-term with intangible long-term results

how managers and leaders tend to operate in them. In the book's later sections, you will see the differences between managers and leaders played out with respect to each of the success factors identified on the left-hand axis of the matrix: competitive strategy/advantage, organizational culture/capability, external/internal change, individual effectiveness/style, and bottom-line performance/results. If you consider yourself more leadership oriented than management oriented, I suggest that you work through Section I, because doing so will give you a good overall feel for the characteristics of the five environment types, and a conceptual framework for approaching the later sections and chapters. If you consider yourself more management oriented, I suggest you begin with a later section or chapter to get you into the practical specifics of the book before returning to this section.

You know, as well as I do, that there is no quick and easy formula for creating your own ultimate capitalistic engine. People manage, people lead, and people, being people, always do so imperfectly. However, I've found myself in hundreds of organizational situations over the years—as a student, as an executive, and as a consultant—and over time I have seen the natural tension between managers and leaders play itself out both wonderfully and disastrously. As I share some of these experiences with you, I hope you'll gain some insights that, more than any faddish formula, will help you tap the power of that tension for your own organization and yourself. First, let's take a closer look at each of the management/leadership environments.

1

Management-Dominated

Management-Dominated Characteristics

Over the past fifteen years or so, one company in the electronics and electric appliance industry (I'll refer to it as Enco) has grown and prospered above the levels of its competitors in the industry. Its growth during this period has been tenfold, while its profits have continued to outshine those of its peers. Enco has accomplished all this by being management-dominated. Now with sales in the several billion dollar range, Enco has become a model not only for its industry, but for companies in other industries as well.

In terms of competitive strategy and advantage, Enco pursues *same-game strategies*, a term coined at the consulting firm of McKinsey & Company to describe strategies that do not change the basic nature and definition of the business in the marketplace. In other words, Enco pursues strategies that look like those of its competitors. However, Enco prides itself on doing the best job of implementing those strategies and enjoys its position as a cost and market leader. Far from trying to change the market or the nature of their business or introduce major innovations, the company focuses instead on low-cost manufacturing capability at particular levels of differentiated quality.

When it comes to organizational culture and capability, Enco strives to perpetuate the culture that it has been developing throughout its history. By this point, the focus on cost and market leadership has become second nature to every manager and worker at Enco. Senior executives submit monthly operating reports that detail growth, profitability, and return on capital and are designed to track the firm's cost and market leadership positions. The culture epitomizes control and the careful tracking of variables that relate to cost and market leadership.

With respect to external and internal change, Enco tries to absorb it quickly in order to avoid disrupting the company's stability too much. Interestingly, Enco has made a string of acquisitions over the years and has spent heavily to develop existing business and build new plants. Interestingly, the basic motive behind these changes, whether they respond to external change or represent a self-developed internal change, has been the desire for stability in terms of growth, profitability, return on capital and general business development. So many goals, objectives, policies, and standards exist within Enco that when change does occur, people know exactly how to factor it into the system. Ironically, even the development of new products reflects a drive toward stability, since the company pursues a set goal of reaping over 20 percent of its sales from new products every year.

In the area of individual effectiveness and style, Enco obviously loves structured approaches and processes because it believes that they will provide the kind of stable effectiveness the company seeks. The CEO spends the bulk of his time reviewing strategic and operating plans versus actuals, the reports submitted each month by division heads. This reflects his strong belief in corporate planning and persistent monitoring, and he requires all his executives and managers to keep intimately involved in this process.

Understandably, Enco looks to its bottom line for tangible results and performance, such as growth, profitability, return on capital, and many other financial, operating, and strategic measures. In fact, Enco expects nothing else from its various divisions and businesses except that they maintain cost and market leadership, both of which are tangible, measurable factors. When operating divisions do not score tangible results, Enco's CEO and staff immediately move to isolate and solve whatever problems have caused the poor performance.

By any sort of objective analysis, Enco has turned in exemplary performance in recent years, with the business press frequently citing it as one of the best run companies in America today.

The Roles of Managers and Leaders in Management-Dominated Environments

In an organization such as Enco, the mind of the manager clearly dominates. The preference for same-game strategies, perpetuating culture, and striving for stability represents a manager orientation, and such a preference leaves little room for leaders, who might march to different drumbeats. When leaders do find their way into this organization, they usually feel stifled, shackled, and even denigrated by the managers. This does not mean that Enco's managers are dull, unimaginative, uncreative people. They're not. But they do confine their imaginations and creativity within structured and prescribed bounds. Managers in management-dominated organizations do a great job developing other managers because there are few distracting ideas or alternatives. The manager's development track is clear and precise, leaving little room for flexibility. This makes the role of managers in such organizations easily communicated and understood.

Management-Dominated Strengths and Weaknesses

Management-dominated organizations, environments and people enjoy numerous strengths. To their credit, organizations such as Enco do become quite adroit at pursuing their strategic directions and achieving competitive advantage in their markets. The best run management-dominated organizations do, in fact, pursue the same game as other competitors, but with more success. In addition, the cultures in management-dominated organizations tend to become very entrenched, which can provide great strength in terms of predictability, constancy, and dependability. People always know the required priorities, objectives, and concerns of the organization, because management so clearly spells out its expectations in structured approaches and processes. This also applies to bottom-line results and clear-cut standards for profitability, growth, and return on capital. When such organizations, environments, and people achieve the stability they crave, they find it easier to weather the storms of change by sticking to their knitting and focusing on the basics. Although they rarely create change for the sake of change, they can and will engineer it to attain stability. Throughout the organization, executives can easily measure and track individual effectiveness, which, again, contributes to stability.

Because management-dominated organizations pay strict attention to the basic elements of business success, they usually understand exactly what they are really trying to accomplish. However, this strength can turn into a deadly weakness whenever same-game strategies no longer work in their industries and markets or if such organizations fail to maintain a market leadership position. Management-dominated organizations such as Enco cannot easily develop new-game strategies or envision a total reconfiguration of an industry or a market. Thus they tend to thrive only in more stable, mature industries where they can pursue same-game strategies.

The ability to perpetuate existing cultures also becomes a weakness whenever a management-dominated organization must change its culture in a major way. If the industry or market changes in a major way or a strong competitor launches a highly successful new-game strategy implemented by a new sort of culture, the management-dominated organization finds it very difficult to respond in kind. While the management-dominated organization can and does change, it does not deal well with extreme change, crisis, or major upheavals. Unfortunately, in these tumultuous times, most industries are experiencing greater levels of change than ever.

Finally, because management-dominated organizations, environments, and people pay scant attention to anything but tangible results and performance, they often fail to seize opportunities for changing an industry or market or creating major new products and services. To grow, they must extend the past and build on existing products and services rather than invent anything revolutionary or radically new.

Benefiting from Management-Dominated Organizations

Despite the weaknesses of management-dominated organizations, their stakeholders can benefit from their orientation. First, individuals working for a management-dominated organization can gain a great deal of satisfaction if they prefer clear-cut policies and formal procedures. The person who is most attuned to the mind of the manager will feel perfectly comfortable in a management-dominated organization. This applies to every position, from entry level to middle management and even the top executive ranks.

In the latter case, an executive in a management-dominated organization should look for industries or market opportunities where same-game strategies will work, where perpetuating the existing culture will be beneficial, where striving for stability makes sense, where structured approaches and processes are effective, and where the focus on tangible short-term results will bring success.

Shareholders, for their part, should carefully monitor whether their management-dominated organization continues to match its unique capabilities with market and growth opportunities. If shareholders see a mismatch in terms of an acquisition or a foray into a new market, they should communicate their observations to the board of directors or consider investing in a different firm. Shareholders benefit most when management domination comes to bear in those areas where it can reap the greatest rewards, namely, doing "more and better" of the same thing it has been doing in the marketplace. If this path is likely to continue, hold on to your investment, if not, sell.

Customers of management-dominated organizations benefit most if they are looking for product and service reliability, quality, and cost-effectiveness because management-dominated organizations really can provide these benefits. Never, however, should customers expect tremendous product innovation or great new dimensions of service because management-dominated organizations seldom deliver these things.

Society at large benefits most when management-dominated organizations align themselves with established, mature industries that enjoy relatively unchanging products and services at competitive costs and at differentiated quality levels. Society does not benefit when such organizations attempt to constrain innovation and new directions that break too much from the past, nor does society benefit when such organizations try to stifle innovative competition or drive it out of the market. No society or economy could function successfully without a healthy number of well-run management-dominated organizations. While such organizations tend to become more bureaucratic, more systematized, and potentially stagnant over time, they do add a measure of stability to a fast-changing world. Still, while they serve their purpose well, management-dominated organizations do not represent the optimum type of organization and therefore will probably not make the most significant contributions to economic and social well-being in the future.

2

Leadership-Driven

Leadership-Driven Characteristics

A rapidly growing high-technology company, SPR (not its real name), with several hundred million dollars in revenue and with a unique way of growing and developing provides a good example of the leadership-driven environment and organization. SPR company produces semiconductors, computer components, instruments, and other high-tech gear. According to experts in the field, this company has racked up an impressive record of earnings growth and will shine in the years ahead. Recognizing that innovation does not come easily to large organizations, SPR creates a separate start-up company for every new product line or extension it undertakes. These units enjoy great autonomy, yet they also benefit from SPR's umbrella. The company has already launched several very successful start-ups and expects to initiate dozens more in the decade ahead.

When I studied SPR within the framework of success factors, it clearly emerged as a leadership-driven organization with leadership-driven people and a leadership-driven environment. In terms of competitive strategy and advantage, it constantly formulates *new-game strategies*. As the whole company pushes toward innovation, it strives to create the right kind of environment for innovation to flourish. SPR's CEO cares less about defending market share than about creating new value and opportunity in the marketplace. Once SPR develops a brand new way of competing or meeting customer needs in the marketplace, it establishes a new business and then moves on to other new-game strategies. As each new business grows larger it pursues a similar path by spawning a second generation of new businesses.

When it comes to organizational culture and capability, SPR creates a new culture for each new product line or extension. In this way, SPR can always align new organizational cultures with the new-game strategies. The CEO says that he would much rather oversee numerous $50 million to $100 million companies than one large billion dollar outfit.

In the area of external and internal change, SPR relishes the crises and chaos that often attend big changes in the marketplace. Nothing energizes SPR more than continual and aggressive change. SPR loves to create change and is constantly in the midst of doing so.

When you consider SPR in terms of individual effectiveness and style, you see any number of its teams operating according to informal and unstructured approaches and processes. The president of each of the created companies has a great deal of responsibility and authority, allowing him or her to change product design, build factories, issue stock, raise money, and hire and fire, using whatever approach works best for that particular product line and company.

Finally, SPR emphasizes intangible long-term bottom-line performance and results, disdaining the rest of the world's concern about quarterly earnings and revenue growth, two measures by which SPR has ironically demonstrated superior performance. The cart, it seems, at least for the present, inevitably follows the horse at SPR. In this case, the "horse" represents providing greater value to the customer, producing products and services to fulfill a crying need neglected by competitors, charting new waters in search of new applications and innovations and generally creating an internal organizational environment that maximizes the creativity and productivity of people affording them unlimited opportunities to explore new product offerings and new market niches. To maintain a healthy horse, SPR pays extreme attention to the long-term viability of each company, the strength of each management team, the fulfillment and satisfaction of all employees, the value the units provide to customers, and last but not least, lasting contributions to society.

The Roles of Managers and Leaders in Leadership-Driven Environments

By definition, a leadership-driven environment offers little recognition of the role of the manager. As a result, managers in such organizations can become extremely frustrated as they find themselves unable to make much headway toward systematizing, structuring and stabilizing things. Leaders within leadership-driven environments, who constantly change everything in sight, find that structured approaches, formal systems, and other stabilizing measures run completely counter to their cultural values. While you might expect to see managers in certain administrative, accounting, and financial positions, even these jobs require a leader's touch because these functional areas change along with everything else within such a leadership-driven environment. Contrary to popular opinion, leaders do know how to manage such mundane things as accounting and personnel functions. They simply approach such functions as leaders — with an eye to overall purpose rather than to specific procedures. Of course, managers do find their way into these kinds of environments and may work in them for a number of years, but leadership-driven environments seldom gain the true benefit of the managerial mind. The leaders tend to put up with a certain amount of managerial influence, but they never fully tap its power. Eventually, managers will leave such environments, out of frustration and a declining sense of self-worth. On the other hand, leaders so greatly stimulate other leaders that the truly leadership-driven environment quickly becomes a haven for leadership-oriented executives and employees.

Leadership-Driven Strengths and Weaknesses

The greatest strengths of these kinds of organizations, environments, and people are their ability to change, innovate, and create. Their vitality is enormous and often stands behind the new markets, new industries, and new products or services that power a successful economy and society. Given their passion for change and dramatic improvement, such organizations remain agile, capable of exploiting conditions that would sink their more stable counterparts. I think this is why we have heard so much about the need for leaders in the past several years. The world changes these days at such an accelerated pace, leaders and leadership-driven environments seem to offer a promising alternative for guiding our organizations and societies successfully into the future.

On the negative side, leadership-driven organizations, environments, and people have trouble maintaining their positions as dominant players for long periods of time. Since they neither do a good job of defending markets over time nor of bringing about the kind of stability that encourages the gradual reduction of costs, the steadily improved delivery of products and services to the customer, and the product and service refinements that help a business mature within an industry, such organizations, environments, and people usually do not handle the maturing stages of the corporate or product life cycle very well. Those that are leadership-driven embark so regularly on new-game strategies that they rarely invest the time or attention in perfecting a given strategy or position over time. To do so would look like pursuing same-game strategies, something leaders shun like the plague. The same holds true of their cultures. As leaders plunge themselves into crisis after crisis, they never build the stable kind of environment that allows for people to learn how to defend market positions when necessary. Sometimes, too, of course, they can suffer from insufficient attention to tangible short-term results.

Not infrequently, leadership-driven organizations do not grow beyond a certain size unless they somehow learn to live with the structure, systems, and processes necessary to maintain a larger organization.

Benefiting from the Leadership-Driven Organization

In our economy and society, the leadership-driven organization fulfills the vital role of breaking with current tradition and past approaches in order to innovate and bring about the breakthroughs that benefit everyone. Such organizations can help us find new solutions to old problems in ways that management-dominated organizations never can. This role demands strong leadership. As an individual within such an organization, you can most benefit by making sure that your own skills and goals tend to coincide with the leadership side of the management/leadership continuum. If they don't, you will probably find it frustrating and unfulfilling to remain inside a leadership-driven organization.

If you work at the executive level, you will probably want to do everything within your power to maintain the company's pure focus on leadership qualities, which may mean keeping the company at an appropriate size. In order to take fuller or additional advantage of breakthroughs, innovations, and truly new ways of thinking about doing business, you may want to form an affiliation or some other kind of creative relationship with an organization that can take the product, service, or new orientation in the marketplace into a more stable management-oriented phase of its life cycle. Doing so, however, is one of the major problems facing American business today: its inability to take advantage of innovations and breakthroughs on many fronts by creating organizations that can effect mass production at low cost and efficiently deliver total service and satisfaction on a wide scale. This road is one less traveled, but we would all benefit from more traffic.

Shareholders desiring to benefit from a leadership-driven organization should look for one that has a track record of breakthroughs and is currently positioned for new breakthroughs and major innovations, and such potential shareholders should pay special attention to industries where innovations will make the most difference. Once a leadership-driven organization achieves a breakthrough, the investor may do well to ensure that, like SPR, the organization can create other leadership-driven organizations or can move agilely on to the next breakthrough. If the organization can do neither, the shareholder may do well to invest elsewhere.

Customers benefit from leadership-driven organizations when they really want and need greater value, innovative breakthroughs, or products and services not offered by other organizations. Customers desiring more stable, less breakthrough value–oriented products or services would do well to look to management-dominated alternatives.

Finally, in terms of society at large, leadership-driven organizations greatly benefit the general population when they can use their orientations toward change, innovation, and breakthroughs to redefine a better future. This can give a society a crucial leading edge in international commerce. However, if the society cannot successfully integrate the leadership-driven organization into its other constituents, it will benefit less. Organizations isolated and separated from the rest of society do not function optimally. Unfortunately, we have not done such a good job in the United States with this type of integration over the last few decades.

3

Conflict-Oriented

Conflict-Oriented Characteristics

Conflict-oriented organizations, environments, and people attempt to apply equal amounts of management and leadership. While striving for this balance, such organizations or people usually end up creating an adversarial environment in which the minds of managers contend and compete with the souls of leaders. In my experience, one such organization, which I'll refer to as Consolidated, is a large consumer products manufacturer with heavy emphasis on superior product marketing throughout the world. In the arena of competitive strategy and advantage, Consolidated attempts to pursue both same-game strategies and new-game strategies. Sometimes it does so by separating more stable, same-game-strategy product lines from the less stable, new-game-strategy ones. Oftentimes Consolidated will try to insulate a new product area from more mature areas of the business, even though it will still keep the new products within the product marketing management structure so that their innovative characteristics can influence the more stable product lines, thus ensuring constant revitalization, or so the thinking goes. However, this usually causes an ongoing struggle between

same-game strategists and new-game strategists. The senior management of Consolidated actually encourages this conflict, arguing
that both points of view must inform any really effective decision.

When it comes to organizational culture and capability, Consolidated, like other conflict-oriented organizations, keeps trying to
change its culture. Culture change is a constant topic of discussion
among the senior team. Since the organization simultaneously pursues same-game strategies and new-game strategies, it naturally
keeps altering its culture. For example, a new product line requires
a leadership-driven culture to generate the excitement necessary to
launch the line. But when the line matures, it needs a more
management-dominated culture to accommodate more orderly
growth. In order to deal with these two requirements, Consolidated
places managers and leaders in head to head competition with each
other to create a supposedly balanced perspective. What results is
conflict, internal politics, and a perpetually provoked culture. I
might refer to it as a *conflict culture*. Consolidated, like other conflict-
oriented organizations, attempts to make leadership-driven subcul-
tures more management-dominated and vice versa.

This situation relates to how conflict-oriented organizations
deal with external and internal change. Typical of this type of organization, Consolidated desires stability and crisis simultaneously.
While the company wants stability for its more stable product lines,
it also fuels crisis to keep the product lines revitalized. The company
uses crisis to disrupt stability and stability to interrupt crisis. The
conflict continues. Again, in the name of balance, the senior team
thinks it must maintain fairly steady conflict between crisis and
stability. By pitting the one perspective against the other, senior
management believe that they can enhance decision making and
improve the overall performance of the organization.

In terms of individual effectiveness and style, Consolidated
prides itself on maintaining an equal emphasis on structured and
unstructured approaches, or what it likes to call loose, tight processes. In those areas of the organization that currently follow new-
game strategies, the approaches and processes tend to be loose, but
tight processes and procedures are constantly being pushed to balance the loose ones. Why? In order to make way for the more stable
same-game strategies. As these conflicts take place, great debates

and heated confrontations often erupt. Still, senior management encourages such conflicts, believing that they strengthen the organization. When it comes to performance and results, Consolidated places equal weight on intangible long-term results and tangible short-term results. Not unexpectedly, this also ignites some fierce competition at Consolidated, with senior management cheering from the sidelines. Senior management feels strongly that such internal competitiveness heightens everyone's awareness of the basic conflict between long-term and short-term goals. Despite this conflict, however, Consolidated fully expects to achieve both.

In the final analysis, conflict-oriented organizations, environments, and people maintain an adversarial, competitive, and conflict-driven environment that encourages managers to wrestle with leaders in an effort to improve overall effectiveness.

The Roles of Managers and Leaders in Conflict-Oriented Environments

Conflict-oriented environments demand both strong managers and forceful leaders. The leaders foster the development of other leaders, while the managers groom other managers, usually in fairly equal numbers. With balance as the watchword, an overabundance of either orientation would tip the scales too far in that direction. Then the debates become too one-sided. For this reason, such organizations want both managers and leaders who will stand their respective grounds, making sure all points of any conflict emerge forcefully and clearly. Thus the management/leadership environment in a conflict-oriented organization remains very adversarial and competitive. The role of the manager is to fight for his or her viewpoint by articulating it well and not backing off when the going gets tough. With the leader's role being similar, it's easy to see how the overriding stimulus in such organizations is to battle for position and persuasion, oftentimes promoting office politics.

Conflict-Oriented Strengths and Weaknesses

The strengths of conflict-oriented organizations, environments, and people derive from their attempts to include both the mind of the manager and the soul of the leader in decision making and action taking. Although the two battle with each other constantly, the conflicts can result in effective decisions. Given the near-equal emphasis on both, such organizations can be both innovative and well managed, both change-oriented and conservative, and viable both in the short term and far into the future. While the managers may not fully appreciate the leaders, and vice versa, they do manage to exist in a workable, albeit conflict-ridden, environment. The constant conflict and competition, however, leads to many of the weaknesses of these kinds of organizations.

Trying to be all things at once by pitting differences against each other can lead to being nothing at all. Often conflict-oriented organizations accomplish neither same-game nor new-game strategies very well. Conflict between the two can erode each of their benefits. Always trying to balance same-game and new-game strategies can lead to mediocrity rather than superiority. The same holds true for such an organization's culture, which seldom becomes as strong as possible because of all the conflict and change. Fights, while productive at times, also can sap your energy. They certainly cost a lot in terms of organizational time and attention, particularly when office politics increase. Conflict-oriented organizations are notorious for sending mixed signals throughout their organizations, affecting and sometimes severing their strategic focus and cultural unity.

In terms of individual effectiveness and style, the managers make the leaders feel uncomfortable, and vice versa. Both feel somewhat guilty about their ingrained perspectives and all the continual conflict. But even so, the managers in conflict-oriented organizations tend to label leaders "flakey" and inattentive to reality and detail, while the leaders think of the managers as mundane, dull, and unimaginative. Finally, the struggle to balance tangible and intangible short-term and long-term results often incurs a heavy price: mediocre results. As with the other success factors, the conflict between managers and leaders makes spectacular results very difficult to attain.

Benefiting from Conflict-Oriented Organizations

The greatest benefit of the conflict-oriented organization comes from the fact that unlike those governed by one orientation or the other, it recognizes the value of both and thus represents a more highly evolved organizational environment. However, its adversarial, conflict-laden balancing act renders it less than optimally effective. For the individual working inside such an organization, success depends on retaining strong managerial or leadership traits and minimizing the potential damage to egos and feelings all the conflict can cause. Gradually, a person can come to appreciate more fully the opposing views without getting angry or upset. Most of all, individuals in such organizations should try to overcome any feelings of guilt about their own orientation. It's not wrong to be a strong manager. And it's not wrong to be a forceful leader.

Likewise, the best way for executives to move themselves and their organizations ahead is to recognize their situation as a developmental one that can evolve into a less conflict-oriented one over time. The executive who understands this can help move the organization in a less adversarial and more integrated and holistic direction.

The conflict-oriented organization results in part from Wall Street's mixed signals between the short term and the long term. Thus shareholders should recognize that conflict-oriented organizations usually produce only average results. Conflict-oriented organizations may offer a modest return on investment but will rarely bring in spectacular earnings. Unfortunately, there are a lot of conflict-oriented organizations in the world, so be sure you know what you're investing in.

As a customer, you will probably get good solid products and services from this kind of company. Their breakthroughs will probably not startle the world, nor will their ability to control and reduce costs. Still, such organizations will consistently prove dependable.

Society at large will benefit from conflict-oriented organizations only if such organizations progress beyond their conflict-orientation and find ways to integrate and balance management and leadership without pitting them against each other.

4

Vacillation-Prone

Vacillation-Prone Characteristics

Vacillation-prone organizations, environments, and people shift wildly between management and leadership emphases, finding it difficult to tap the power of either. As a rule, they suffer from doubt, uncertainty, and a lack of identity and clear direction.

One such organization for which I consulted is a large retailing chain, which to protect client confidentiality I'll refer to as Glendale's. Glendale's has pursued nothing but reactive strategies over the past twenty years. When industry leaders introduced innovative new in-store concepts and merchandising methods, Glendale's followed suit aggressively. Then, as other industry leaders tightened executive control and urged campaigns of cost containment, Glendale's did the same. It could lead, and it could manage, but its motivation to do one or the other never sprang from internal sources, always coming about instead as a reaction to events in the marketplace. There should have been a revolving door on the CEO's office, because each wild swing brought with it a new top manager or leader. The company's culture revolved in kind, with Glendale's top executives confusing their people by continually vacillating among the various "capabilities of the day." When the firm picked up an innovative in-store merchandising concept, it substantially changed the internal image of its stores. But then, when it went into a control mode that required abandoning some of the new merchandising concept, it sent completely opposite signals to its people. This kind of on-again/off-again pattern, for the last two decades, has made Glendale's culture virtually schizophrenic.

Reacting to external changes in the marketplace that created much internal confusion and change, Glendale's recently experienced tremendous bouts of stagnation and crisis. A few years ago, the chain's cost-containment policy reduced the number of staff and warehouse personnel to the point that customers began complaining about out-of-stock items and terrible service. While the chain did reduce costs substantially, it also built up a reputation for being unresponsive to customers, a reputation that almost ran Glendale's out of business. In the nick of time, however, a new CEO clambered aboard with bold new ideas. Glendale's picked up some steam again, but then it almost died attempting to assimilate the crisis environment created by the new executive team.

In terms of individual effectiveness and style, Glendale's systems, processes, and general approach to business have been just as uncertain as everything else, moving from formal and structured to informal and unstructured and back again in response to a variety of perceived demands. This inconsistency and uncertainty has seriously compromised the individual effectiveness and productivity of employees and has caused them to wonder what works and what doesn't.

As a result of all its vacillation, Glendale's has turned in marginal or negative performances for several years. It is unable to achieve consistent tangible or intangible results. Today the company barely hangs on as it struggles to understand how it should view its future.

The Roles of Managers and Leaders
in Vacillation-Prone Environments

Managers who assume power within vacillation-prone environments usually try to "kill off" any remnant leaders. Likewise, leaders who gain power try to remove any remaining managers. Not only does an "either/or" attitude dominate the relationship between managers and leaders, but no one even tries, as in conflict-oriented environments, to use the conflict to hammer out more effective decisions. Rather, in vacillation-prone environments, managers and leaders despise each other for destroying the organization. As one regime replaces another, confusion reigns supreme.

Any manager or leader who wants to change this destructive pattern within a vacillation-prone environment must assume the role of peacemaker between the opposing forces, orientations, and people, trying to impose a balanced and integrated perspective that will keep the organization from forever recycling itself on a downward spiral until it ceases to exist. However, sometimes the only way a vacillation-prone environment can evolve into a balanced and integrated one is by first becoming management dominated or leadership driven, thus bringing an end to the harmful recycling.

Vacillation-Prone Strengths and Weaknesses

Vacillation-prone organizations, environments, and people display few, if any, strengths, unless you count the fact that they have, at one time or another, practiced both management and leadership, giving them at least some basis for deciding which orientation to embrace for the future. On the other hand, the weaknesses become painfully obvious. Reactive strategies have never worked for organizations or people over time because they represent only knee-jerk impulsive attempts to duplicate what somebody else is doing in the marketplace. Such strategies may work momentarily, but they cannot sustain life in the long term. Reactive executives seldom think through their strategies as completely as the people who designed them in the first place. Confused cultures developing confused organizational capabilities set records for poor productivity as people enter and exit the company through an ever-revolving door.

Vacillation-prone environments quite often succumb to either stagnation or chaos. Given their reactive nature and confused culture, such environments can move quickly from stability to debilitating stagnation or from crisis to destructive chaos. Likewise, people tend to find the uncertain approaches and processes totally incomprehensible and inconsistent and thus never feel confident about their direction. Commitment levels are consequently low and unstable. The ultimate weakness, of course, comes from the marginal results that usually keep the organization, environment, or person teetering on the brink of survival. While vacillation-prone organizations come in many shapes and sizes, their doubt and uncertainty usually create a death spiral from which they cannot easily recover.

Benefiting from Vacillation-Prone Organizations

To benefit from a vacillation-prone organization, you must help it change. If you are an individual working for such an organization, carefully weigh your ability to change it. If you lack the skill, patience, determination or position, you should probably seek another work environment. The same holds true for executives. To pull out of the death spiral, the organization must be guided to one of the other management/leadership environments. As mentioned earlier, moving to a management-dominated or leadership-driven environment seems to be most viable for such organizations.

Investors or shareholders may want to find a way to buy sufficient stock to control such an organization and bring about the necessary changes. You can often buy vacillation-prone organizations at bargain prices, so if you enjoy the means and relish the challenge of undertaking such a task, you may harvest significant fruit in the long run. Otherwise, you should probably sell your shares at the most opportune moment. Also, vacillation-prone organizations make great leveraged buy-outs because assets are often undervalued and underutilized.

As a customer, you should not expect much in the way of quality or service from vacillation-prone organizations. However, depending on where the pendulum stands at a given moment, you may find some unique value at low prices. Vacillation-prone organizations stay alive by making good reactive moves from time to time, but they frequently also make a like number of poor reactive moves. Watch out for the lemons.

Lastly, society does not benefit at all from such organizations. In fact, they are such sources of frustration and mediocre products, services, and performance that they do little but drain the economy. Society would be better off if such organizations either changed or went out of business, sooner, rather than later.

5

Balanced and Integrated

Balanced and Integrated Characteristics

The most optimally performing organizations, environments, and people are balanced and integrated because they value management, leadership, and the variations in between. They solve the equation for success by relying on management plus leadership. Such organizations and people know how to blend and integrate a wide variety of management and leadership skills into one cohesive whole, in which each individual and each orientation can make a unique contribution to success.

Very few organizations have achieved this state, but I was fortunate enough to get inside one of them not long ago. Freemans, as I'll call it, is a well-known publishing and communications company that approaches the issue of competitive strategy and advantage with what I call *changing-game strategies*. Changing-game strategies are strategies that take into account the fluid nature of the marketplace, the industry, the competition, suppliers, customers, society, and the global economy. Freemans assumes that the game is always changing and, therefore, so must its strategies. Companies such as Freemans always look for all the ways in which the marketplace is changing so that they can blend their refining and revolutionizing orientations appropriately. I witnessed this firsthand at Freemans when the company moved from publishing magazines and newspapers into state-of-the-art networks and electronic information services, all the result of changing-game strategies. They did this by strategically planning and strategically experimenting so that the experiments improved planning and vice versa. For example, Freemans experimented with having traditional newspaper and magazine reporters prepare stories for both print and electronic information services. The experiment worked beautifully, stimulating reporters and maximizing resources. This led to further integration of print and electronic news dissemination operations.

When it comes to organizational culture and capabilities, Freemans has steadily renewed its culture to take full advantage of changing circumstances in the marketplace and to prepare its people with the capabilities they need to respond appropriately to change. As a result of its changing-game strategic posture, Freemans has woven the electronics side of the business into the fabric of its entire culture, helping even cub reporters keep abreast of changing technology. Changing-game strategies do not attempt to hold things in place for the purposes of stability, nor do they create a crisis environment. Instead, they emphasize renewal and the ongoing search for new insights into the nature of the marketplace among executives and employees at all levels. The reason Freemans is able to renew its culture rather than just perpetuate it, create a new one, change it, or confuse it is because all culture renewals are based on the root values and capabilities of the old culture that remain constant, albeit constantly applied in new ways over time. In this way, the culture doesn't experience change, but rather reapplication or renewal. A good example is the new application of Freemans' recognized high quality of news reporting in the information services arena with the same human resources and cultural values.

Freemans blends its need for both stability and crisis in a way that makes change easy for its people to anticipate and handle. Stability never deteriorates into stagnation, crisis never escalates into chaos. Rather, Freemans taps the natural tension between the two by blending stability and crisis into an ever-evolving dynamic environment. Change in this kind of environment is not abrupt or absent or abnormal—it is fluid and ongoing. Freemans' move into electronic information services has been graceful and enduring. There has been no resistance from people, and the change has been linked to all aspects of the organization. Change at Freemans is created, anticipated, and responded to as a normal part of the organization's culture.

In terms of individual effectiveness and style, Freemans retains highly dynamic approaches and processes, modifying them when necessary but never tossing aside existing standards without good reason. The company's formal and informal systems do not compete with each other, but rather complement one another. This promotes personal development of workers and imbues everyone with an ability to value different and even opposing perspectives. The emphasis, again, is on integration, communication, and understanding. The company's attitude toward individual effectiveness is one of continually expanding the boundaries of excellence by improving approaches and processes. As a result, people are very comfortable looking for better ways to meet customer information needs, increase commitment to journalistic standards of excellence, or seize opportunities to move the organization ahead.

In terms of bottom-line performance and results, balanced and integrated organizations combine tangible with intangible and short-term with long-term results, so that their people cannot talk about one without talking about the other. For example, when it became clear that Freemans should plunge more fully into electronic information services, it did so, after successful experimentation, on a broad front, not just with a restricted set of people or a new division. While the executive team knew that this would drain short-term earnings from the traditional newspaper and magazine businesses, they also knew that this short-term sacrifice would buy longer-term growth and development for the whole corporation.

Freemans also places great stock in its reputation, an intangible result that resists quantification. Yet, as the company has grown, it has consistently cashed in on this asset by moving into carefully selected fields on the strength of its long-standing reputation, always renewing and reinforcing the reputation along the way.

Freemans more carefully integrates management and leadership than most companies. Some observers have remarked that the organization doesn't move fast enough, while others have at times criticized it for moving too fast. In reality, Freemans moves at its own well-chosen speed, tapping the natural tension between the mind of the manager and the soul of the leader. The difference between Freemans and a conflict-oriented organization often defies clear, quantitative analysis because Freemans' orientation is more of an attitude and a feeling that permeates the entire organizational environment. There is a deep valuing of differing perspectives and orientations, a solid commitment to openness and candor in all communications and interactions, and an aggressive willingness to face up to realities and issues in order to positively address and resolve them, no matter how sticky or difficult they are to deal with. Environments such as Freemans' exude a feeling of empowerment, fulfillment, peace, and enduring progress.

The Roles of Managers and Leaders in Balanced and Integrated Environments

Both managers and leaders in balanced and integrated organizations develop their strengths and talents to the fullest while recognizing and appreciating each others' differing talents and strengths. Both think holistically, exploiting the natural tension between them to tie innovation and creativity to analysis and systemization. In other words, managers don't stifle leaders, fight with them, or try to drive them out of the organization. Rather they seek to blend their own skills with those of the leaders. Such blending into a whole makes dealing with change, strategic thinking, and cultural renewal always fluid and smooth. The development orientation is one that encourages each employee, supervisor, or executive to further develop and enhance his or her unique perspectives, orientations, skills, and talents while placing these unique capabilities in the context of the whole. In this way, both managers and leaders are able to see how their capabilities fit into the fabric of the whole group, thus directing their attention and shaping their attitudes toward complementing, blending and integrating. It is this attitude of balance and integration that removes the conflict and taps the power of the tension between managers and leaders.

Balanced and Integrated Strengths and Weaknesses

The strengths of such organizations, environments, and people are substantial. For example, changing-game strategies are consistent with the way the marketplace really works. Thus the optimal organization can continually uncover new insights and develop strategies accordingly. Nothing does more to sustain long-term competitive advantage. In terms of organizational culture and capability, since the integrated, balanced organization continually renews its culture, it perpetuates its beneficial, lasting, and important aspects while at the same time adding well-considered new elements without visiting excessive change or confusion on its people. Such an organization functions like a continuously adapting organism rather than one that is haphazard and variable, buffeted by changes beyond its control.

Balanced and integrated organizations benefit from intertwining stability and crisis into a dynamic environment. If you were to graph change or improvement over time for each of the organizations we have discussed, the management-dominated organization would change the least, favoring stability all the time, while the leadership-driven organization would change most dramatically, favoring constant crisis and change. The conflict-oriented organization would begin to approach the smooth curve of the balanced and integrated renewal pattern, but with less positive improvement and more negative downturns, while the vacillation-prone organization's line would jump all over the place, mostly on the negative side.

Dynamic development permeates the area of individual effectiveness and style for balanced and integrated organizations, which blend existing with improving approaches to push forward the boundaries of excellence, always evolving better ways of doing things and exploiting the natural tension between the manager's mind and the leader's soul.

Of course, balanced and integrated organizations realize peak performances in both tangible and intangible areas. Companies such as General Electric, PepsiCo, Hewlett Packard, Dow Jones, and Corning maintain positive and profitable performance levels over long periods of time, indicating their justifiable claims as balanced and integrated organizations.

Utopias may exclude imperfections and weaknesses, but in the real world, no utopia currently exists. Even the most optimal organization will not perform perfectly in every situation. For example, a leadership-driven organization can sometimes introduce major innovations more rapidly than a balanced and integrated one, and a management-dominated organization can, on occasion, do a better job of defending the market position of a mature business than can any other. However, although balanced and integrated organizations may not provide the best solution to an immediate business problem, such organizations will, by the law of averages, win far more often than they lose, thus propelling themselves to the top ranks of organizational performers.

Another weakness, if you can call it that, is the fact that you cannot create such an organization easily. Most progress through a conflict-oriented stage before approaching the balanced and integrated realm. The process can be painful and time consuming, and it usually requires a strong commitment and clear vision at the senior executive level. The differences between conflict-oriented and balanced and integrated organizations are often subtle and require firm resolve on the part of everyone in the organization to move beyond conflict and competition toward balance and integration. However, if those at the top really want lasting, superior performance in terms of the empowerment, fulfillment, and satisfaction of their people, as well as the highest levels of productivity, quality, and customer loyalty, the results will certainly be worth the price.

Benefiting from Balanced and Integrated Organizations

Every stakeholder benefits from more balanced and integrated organizations. Yes, other kinds of organizations may get the job done quite well from time to time, but this optimal organization will create greater and more lasting value for everyone with whom it comes in contact. If you are an individual working for a balanced and integrated organization, steadfastly develop your own particular perspectives while always placing them in the context of the whole, with an eye to integrating them with those who differ from you.

If you are an executive, foster the development of both managers and leaders. Keep a balanced and integrated perspective at all times and you will see yourself, your team, and your organization prosper. It may be hard to build a balanced and integrated organization, but it is quite easy for an executive to give the effort daily attention.

If you are a shareholder, hold onto your stock. It will be one of the best long-term investments you can ever make. These stocks will weather recessions, depressions, and other traumas, unlike the others.

For society, balanced and integrated organizations represent the model of how people, organizations, nations, races, and all human endeavor can work together for the benefit of the whole. All participants can contribute to making this world and their lives better, more fulfilled, more productive, and more enlightened. Balanced and integrated organizations may represent an ideal, but I think they stand as the organizations of the future.

II

Competitive Strategy/ Advantage

Strategic management will continue to receive a great deal of attention from businesspeople in the future, especially with such issues as quality, service, cost, and innovation becoming more and more critical for companies that compete in the intensely competitive global environment. Strategic management will continue to play a critical role in helping managers and leaders allocate their direct resources and determine the directions of their organizations. Many organizations, however, will have trouble reaching agreement on strategic issues because their managers and leaders hold such fundamentally different ideas about strategic management.

Many options will play themselves out in the different types of organizations. Management-dominated organizations will generally pursue same-game strategies and a head-on, do-it-better-than-our-competitors approach. Leadership-driven organizations will invent new-game strategies, designed for innovation and break-throughs. Conflict-oriented organizations will try to balance the two, creating an environment of conflict, while vacillation-prone organizations will reactively shift from one to the other without quite knowing for sure which is right. Only balanced and integrated organizations will succeed in exploiting the benefits of both the management and leadership points of view. Unlike their less highly evolved counterparts, balanced and integrated organizations will develop changing-game strategies that act and respond fluidly to the dynamics of the marketplace. In such organizations, managers and leaders will surely obtain different insights into different per-spectives, and both will try to answer the same strategic question: Can you anticipate changes in customer needs, competitor actions, and the ways in which your company can fully exploit its strengths in the future?

In this section you will see the basic orientations of managers and leaders play themselves out in the arena of strategy and com-petitive advantage. In the process you'll see some ways in which any organization can tap the natural tension between the two view-points and thereby take steps toward creating a more balanced and integrated organization.

6

Strategy plus Culture

Managers Concentrate on Strategies; Leaders Nurture Cultures

While both managers and leaders may recognize the value of both strategy and culture in an organization, managers tend to think of the strategy-culture mix from the strategic perspective, while leaders tend to see the mix from the cultural side. This happens because strategy lends itself to analysis, the systematic generation of alternatives, and calculated decision making. Culture, on the other hand, involves inspiration, value sharing, and deep sensitivity to capabilities. By nature, the manager's mind favors clear-cut courses of action based on the implementation of a specific, detailed plan to resolve an issue. The leader's soul, on the other hand, naturally favors creating a cultural climate and attitude conducive to resolving an issue through an appropriate course of action. While strategy deals with the hard S's of McKinsey's 7S model—strategy, structure, and systems—culture involves the soft S's—staff, skills, style, and superordinate goals or shared values.

Not long ago a large electric utility in the eastern United States began transforming itself from a defensive, regulation-conscious organization to a more offensive, market-oriented one. The whole electric utility industry had been going through a lot of change as increased competition and alternative sources of electricity made the once monopolistic domination of most utilities a thing of the past. During the course of this transformation, the company in question had undertaken several acquisitions, and in order to digest the new units, the parent firm soon found it necessary to inaugurate a program of down-sizing and staff reduction in its many divisions and subsidiaries. One of the divisions, a commercial distribution unit struggling with how to make its own strategy more competitive and its own culture more conducive to marketing while at the same time trying to make them fit with the entire company's strategy and culture, asked that I help them solve the problem.

During a day-long session with the commercial division's management team, I quickly saw two dominant and distinctive points of view emerging. One point of view, articulated by a manager named John, maintained that the division should worry primarily about crystallizing, clarifying, and documenting a comprehensive strategy for the division based on the company's new direction and philosophy of diversification and market competitiveness. John felt that the division's improved performance would rest firmly on a clear-cut strategy that laid out exactly how the division would serve customers, position itself against a growing number of competitors, and further develop existing division strengths, such as customer responsiveness and system reliability.

The other emerging point of view, articulated by Tony, insisted that the commercial division should work primarily on creating and nurturing the kind of corporate culture required by the company's new direction and philosophy, namely, one that emphasized marketing and customer-service skills. Tony blamed the division's mediocre performance on apprehension and uncertainty among employees over the company's future. These feelings, he felt, had developed because of the recent changes, misfires, and layoffs imposed by corporate headquarters. Obviously, then, it made sense to involve all employees in establishing a new working environment characterized by market sensitivity and strategic awareness, skills and attitudes they currently lacked.

As I probed further into these two dominant viewpoints, an intriguing insight surfaced. While the two men clearly cared deeply about their organization and could argue their positions without coming to blows, neither really heard what the other was saying. John could not see how focusing on the working environment or culture would solve the problem, and Tony could not accept the possibility that a strategy-driven course of action would alter the deep-seated uncertainty, mistrust, and confusion caused by downsizing and layoffs in both the commercial division and the company as a whole. It was a standoff.

Further discussion revealed that such standoffs frequently occurred in staff meetings, with groups fairly consistently choosing up sides, the managers on one side and the leaders on the other. After I initiated a rather lengthy discussion about the differences between managers and leaders, which ignited a lot of emotion on both sides, someone asked the question "Who's right?"

"You tell me," I said. Then I led the whole group through two exercises designed to help them answer their own question.

Zigging When You Should Be Zagging

First, I sketched out a hypothetical situation. Suppose a company with a fragmented, weak, confused culture decides to resolve the situation with an elaborate and sophisticated strategy that will presumably force the company to come to grips with culture issues as part of strategy implementation. For example, a company with low morale and a lack of confidence in senior management decides to initiate a major strategic positioning assessment. I called this approach *zigging*. I asked the division managers, "What would happen in such a situation?" Tony and other culture fans quickly cited reasons why zigging would never work in a situation that called for *zagging* (i.e., culture building). Interestingly, the strategists reluctantly agreed that the company could encounter difficulties implementing any strategy with a fragmented and unsupportive culture. However, John argued that this would only happen with a virtually dead culture, whereas a mediocre culture could grow while implementing a strict strategy. At this point, Tony strongly disagreed, claiming that only an already strong culture that was completely compatible with the proposed strategy could implement that strategy successfully.

Both sides stuck by their prejudices. The strategists insisted that culture could and should be shaped as a result of implementing a strategy designed to satisfy customer needs, sustain competitive advantage, and capitalize on company strengths (i.e., culture is a byproduct of strategy), and the culturalists argued that strategy should grow out of culture.

"Okay," I said, temporarily tabling the dispute. "Let's try another exercise."

Zagging When You Should Be Zigging

I then presented another hypothetical situation. A company with a strong, ingrained, and highly effective organizational culture finds itself in a mature industry and market that suddenly enters a new phase of restructuring, renewal, and change. In response, the company embarks on a path to strengthen, deepen, and further ingrain the characteristics and elements of its strong culture (zagging) to ensure that it withstands the market changes. In other words, the company facing major external market changes decides to undertake a culture-building program. This time, as you might expect, John and other strategy-oriented managers immediately criticized such a company for burying its head in the sand and attempting to live off past successes. Only a solid, well-implemented strategy, they proclaimed, would save the day in this situation. Of course, Tony disagreed, promoting the fact that a strengthening of the existing culture could include new ways to apply the culture in the context of a changing market. "Aha!" shouted one strategy-minded manager, "That's nothing but a new strategy!" Grudgingly, Tony conceded the point that, yes, the situation did call for a new strategy for applying the culture in a changing market. "But that's just splitting hairs." The dispute raged on until, finally, I asked the group to address the original question, "Who's right?"

Blending Strategy and Culture

At this point, an amazing thing occurred. While discussing the need for an objective evaluation of whether the division should concentrate on strategy or culture, the group slowly reached a consensus — and with no little excitement. One manager summed it up nicely by saying, "Hey, we've been thinking 'either/or' all day. Why not think 'plus' instead? I mean, is there a law against zigging and zagging at the same time?"

During the next couple of hours, the group concluded that a first-stage effort lasting twelve to eighteen months should focus on clarifying and redefining the division's culture and then obtaining all the employees' commitment to it. This would involve a clarification and solidification of the division's and the company's values as they relate to the division's common purpose or mission, unique or distinctive competence, and consistent practices. These values would then be used to rebuild and revitalize the culture. An overlapping second stage, commencing in six months and lasting twelve months, could step up an emphasis on strategy. With the values coming into place and being embraced, the division could then use them in deciding exactly how to respond to competitive market forces and the changing needs of its electricity customers.

The emergence of this consensus taught both sides the value of more deeply appreciating each other's respective viewpoints in an attempt to weld strategy and culture together. Each should play an important, ongoing role, sustaining the other's efforts. By the end of the day, every person in the group felt that he or she had gained an important new insight into the relationship between strategy and culture.

Unfortunately, not all conflicts or disagreements end this way. However, if managers and executives could step outside their prejudices more often, replacing *either/or* with *plus* thinking, they would find it easier to grapple with all the myriad organizational questions that demand a mixture of strategy and culture. Organizations need to emphasize both, but few seem to do so adroitly. Every organization needs to blend strategy and culture, to different degrees at different times, sometimes more greatly emphasizing one or the other, but never at the expense of each other. A culture-deficient organization needs an extra stress on culture, without totally forgetting about strategy, while a strategy-deficient organization requires just the opposite. An organization deficient in both will probably need a strong emphasis on culture to establish the organization, while an organization strong in both will probably need a greater emphasis on strategy to perpetuate the organization.

In conclusion, whatever the needs of your own organization, stay away from knee-jerk judgments. Stimulate *plus*-type thinking, and remember that managers deserve respect for being strategy-driven and leaders deserve respect for being culture-driven. This will help you build a more balanced and integrated organization that is capable of successfully developing and implementing changing-game strategies.

7

Danger plus Opportunity

Managers Consider Dangers; Leaders Sense Opportunities

Imagine entering a room for the first time. Do your eyes gravitate toward its design and layout or toward its contents? Whichever you naturally look at first tends to form your dominant impression, and like most first impressions, your initial viewpoints or opinions are hard to change.

In a time of strategic repositioning, managers and leaders see things very differently. While the soul of the leader usually feels exhilarated by the opportunities inherent in such a situation, the mind of the manager considers the threats and dangers involved. Initially, the leader's view excludes the dangers, while the manager's view excludes the opportunities. This does not mean that leaders are reckless or that managers are timid. Strong leaders certainly can and do consider dangers, weighing the pros and cons, but they first sense the opportunities. The same holds true for good managers, who can and do consider opportunities, but not before reacting first to the dangers. It's a question of emphasis and priority.

A major snack food company employed two highly effective group product managers, each responsible for one of the company's premier product lines, who beautifully illustrated the different ways managers and leaders look at strategic business positions. Both did their jobs extremely well, but in very different ways.

Looking at Dangers Down the Road

The group product manager who looked, first and foremost, at dangers down the road headed the product marketing functions for the company's largest and most profitable product, potato chips. I'll refer to her as Susan. Her group had long been the company's "bread and butter," and Susan had managed over the years to defend its market share flawlessly. Susan was a master at surveying the competition, always ferreting out potential threats or dangers to her own company's position. She also displayed great sensitivity to customers' desires for new variations of the product, and she had successfully introduced a number of product line extensions and variations. A champion market defender, Susan could play the same game as competitors, but always better.

Highly pleased with Susan's performance, the company's top executives planned to promote her to vice president of marketing. Then everyone involved in the company's marketing functions would report to her, including the other product managers.

Since I had conducted a recent management retreat for the company, the president asked me how I felt about the proposed move. I told him I thought it was a bad idea. Surprised by my reaction, he asked me to explain. Before I tell you what I told him, let me describe the other key group product manager.

Sensing Opportunities Ahead

Bob sensed opportunities first and foremost. His responsibilities included the company's newest and most rapidly growing products, the "single serve" product group, which, to many people in the company, represented the company's future. Bob seemed gifted at identifying opportunities for growth in his group, and while his group had not come close to the profit levels of the mainstay group, it promised to do so once it moved past the costly development stage. Bob foresaw endless opportunities for capturing customers' taste buds with new kinds of snack foods, each one of which could become a "bread and butter" product. Restlessly searching for new opportunities, he hardly ever thought about defending current market share positions. Bob was a genius at innovation and change, constantly developing new-game strategies that took competitors by surprise.

I had experienced, first hand, both the opportunity-oriented and the danger-oriented strategic thinking of these two people. In addition, I had observed that neither could communicate very well with the other. Bob saw Susan as restrictive and narrow; Susan thought Bob was too wild and free-wheeling.

The Best of Both Views

Without question, companies need both Susan's and Bob's approach to strategic thinking, particularly when, as in this instance, a company finds itself simultaneously defending market positions while exploring new ones. However, attempting to blend the opportunity and the danger orientations in one person seldom works. The best you can hope for is an appreciation of the two by seasoned executives at the top. Therefore, I told the president that I thought he would make a grave mistake if he placed Bob, the opportunity-oriented leader, in a position where he would report to Susan, the danger-oriented manager. I cited three reasons. First, Susan's skills, competence, and ability made undeniable sense when it came to the company's "bread and butter" product line. You wouldn't want to change that. Second, it would take three to four years of growth and experience for Susan to become more appreciative of the opportunity-orientation and thus effectively fulfill more senior, general management duties. The company couldn't afford for Susan to make that shift right now. Third, Susan's very strength would seriously compromise Bob's effectiveness in the short term.

Therefore, I suggested to the president that he himself could best assume the integrated general management perspective in the short term to ensure the strength and depth of each group product manager's orientation in handling their respective duties. I then asked, "Why not make both the group product managers vice presidents of marketing, one over stable, existing product lines and the other over new and emerging ones?" The president took this advice and made the necessary promotions and organizational changes. Several months later, he reported that the change was working beautifully.

Whenever an organization can benefit from both the danger and opportunity orientations, it should maximize the depth, intensity, and unique perspectives of each. Attaining and maintaining such intensity and depth usually requires encouraging both managers and leaders to further enhance their inherent propensities. When one or the other emerges as a candidate for senior or general management, the organization must allow a long enough transition period for the integration of the two orientations to become complete. In the end, the general manager will probably rely on old habits, still sensing either danger or opportunity first, but he or she will appreciate the need to add the other perspective immediately. In this case, one plus one clearly adds up to three.

8

Version plus Vision

Managers Follow Versions; Leaders Pursue Visions

After someone broadly conceptualizes and envisions a future state of being with a *vision*, someone else often tries to create the desired state with a *version* of that vision. For example, a visionary leader may conceptually define a future for his or her growing hotel chain that delivers exceptional guest services and quality accommodations. This leader's vision becomes so real that he or she can almost taste, smell, and feel what such a future would be like. Now someone could use any of several alternative versions of this vision to achieve that future. One version might involve focusing on the economy-minded market, another on the resort market, another on regional areas, and yet another on high-end trophy hotels. Versions of the vision, in terms of services, also would abound. The versions must complement the vision, of course.

Companies need both visions and versions. Quite naturally, leaders feel most comfortable thinking about, talking about, and pursuing a vision of point Z, while managers just as naturally feel uncomfortable with such thinking and prefer to concentrate on exactly how to get from point *A* to point *Z*. The best leaders can make a future state of being come alive for themselves and others. However, as soon as the vision becomes clear to the best managers, they want to define a version of it for implementation. When they ask, "Exactly how do we create this state?" the leader usually offers little help. In reality, as long as the vision becomes a reality, the leader doesn't worry excessively about which version the managers select. Once managers do select an implementation version, however, they sometimes run into problems. If they ask the leader, who could be unaware of the importance of versions to managers, what to do, they may hear a suggestion to consider other versions. While this doesn't violate the vision for the leader, it usually buffaloes managers, who have forged an inexorable link between the leader's vision and their particular version of it. This problem crops up time and again in organizations, a fact brought home vividly by an entrepreneur who never fully grasped the difference between the two. He had build a small business empire of retailing and manufacturing companies by acquiring one after another.

Mark Daniels (not his real name) was a strong leader, a true visionary who had acquired so many small businesses over a period of ten years that he was actually running a miniconglomerate he hoped would prosper into a world-class corporation. While everyone throughout the company's operations seemed both aware of and supportive of his vision, few of his people could see any rhyme or reason behind Daniels' acquisitions. He would acquire one kind of company one month, communicating that it would provide an important building block for future acquisitions, and then a few months later he would acquire two totally unrelated firms. This confused the management team, who would work hard to develop a strategy for incorporating a group of related companies only to see their work discarded as the entrepreneur flew off in another direction. As the miniconglomerate gathered mass and the subsidiary companies became more and more diverse, the management team wallowed in confusion and uncertainty about their leader's seemingly shifting vision. For his part, Daniels could see his vision as constant and unchanging, but he couldn't see that he was driving many of his managers crazy.

Vision Without Version

I became involved with the company not at Daniels' request, but at the request of Bill Waters (not his real name), the executive vice president, who had decided to leave the company if things didn't change. As Bill put it, "You're my last hope for talking sense into the boss." Over the last six months, not only had the company's chief financial officer, vice president of marketing, and a subsidiary president resigned, but the managements of two key subsidiaries were trying to buy their companies back. In addition, the financial performance of the overall operation had been declining steadily over the last two years. According to Waters, Daniels seemed oblivious to the situation and refused to listen to any suggestions that might compromise his vision. "I've built this company into a $500 million business because I've held fast to a vision," he'd often say, "and nothing is going to distract me from it now." Sticking to a particular version of accomplishing the vision made no sense to him. Anyone who suggested otherwise, he seemed to feel, could just go work somewhere else. This applied to me as well, it turned out.

Not only did Daniels reject all my advice, he suggested that I and all other consultants contribute little to society and should go out and get "real jobs." Not long after my quick exit from the company, Bill Waters followed on my heels.

I stayed in touch with Bill, who went on to run a small manufacturing company but continued to watch the entrepreneur's saga from the sidelines. When Daniels eventually merged his miniconglomerate with another large company and became CEO of the combined organization, I began wondering whether I should get a "real job" and put an end to this consulting business. However, my confidence got a healthy boost about eighteen months later when I read that Daniels' board of directors had ousted him from the CEO slot, even though he controlled a lot of stock. The board cited declining earnings and Daniels' inability to integrate and coordinate the company's farflung operations as primary reasons for his ouster. Vision without attention to version had led to Daniels' fall.

Version Without Vision

The story doesn't end here, however. Bill Waters felt so disgusted with his former boss and the situation that he vowed he would never again get buffaloed by the "vision thing." After approximately three years in his new position, Bill invited me to lunch, which turned into a sad but not surprising confession session. Admitting to having overreacted by refusing to fall victim to a grand vision for his manufacturing company, he had followed a specific plan, set in concrete, that would guarantee no repetition of his experience with Daniels. Now he wanted help. His company was teetering on the brink of bankruptcy. Yes, he had kept the company on a clearly marked path, but with little sense of where it was ultimately heading. There just wasn't any life in the company. He talked about how he wished he could use a dash of his former boss's enthusiasm to ignite his troops. "How," he asked, "can I imbue my company with some of that without creating a monster?"

At the end of our lunch, I agreed to conduct a series of strategic vision sessions with his management group, in which we would attempt to fill the "vision void" that had developed over the last few years. In the process, Bill loosened up his iron-fisted grip on the strategic version of implementation he had narrowly pursued, recognizing it as a paralyzing and deadening approach. Together with his management team, he developed a broader, longer-term vision for the company that the management team then translated into carefully staged versions for implementation. This allowed everyone in the company to see where they were going and soon brought added new life and meaning to their daily activities. In the end, a combination of vision and version began breathing new life into the company. The company barely avoided bankruptcy and soon began slowly but surely ascending an upward track.

Make Sure You've Got Both Vision and Version

Without belaboring the point, a company needs both visioning and versioning activities to sustain it day by day and over the long haul.

Too many people in organizations continue to focus on one at the expense of the other. If you are a leader, make sure you afford managers the opportunity to pursue their versions. If you are a manager, make sure the version you are pursuing reflects a vision, and try to remain open-minded when another version may be required.

9

Isolate plus Correlate

Managers Isolate; Leaders Correlate

Managers naturally *isolate* variables, problems, issues, or concerns in an effort to deal with them individually. In other words, the manager's mind works to separate a problem of product quality from a problem of product image, attempting to solve one at a time. Consequently, managers spend time looking at their organization as a collection of individual and, to some extent, independent variables. In the extreme, this sort of tendency leads to a separated or fragmented view of an organizational environment. Although managers may not consciously dissociate some elements of their organization from others, the very act of isolating variables inevitably brings about such dissociation. Of course, the isolation of variables can enhance certain types of problem solving, allowing managers to strip away unrelated issues and problems and really get to the heart of a problem. In fact, one of the hallmarks of a good manager is his or her ability to slice away symptoms and tangential issues and strike at the causes of problems. "Which variable," asks the manager, "must I control more carefully?"

At the other end of the spectrum, the leader naturally correlates variables, problems, issues, or concerns because that assembles the whole picture. The leader's soul draws product quality and product image together with product profitability, attempting to solve the collection of problems in a holistic way. To the leader's way of thinking, no one variable operates independently from the host of others. This sort of correlation of variables also enhances certain types of problem solving because it enables leaders to see how all the elements of a problem relate to and interact with one another.

These two orientations were readily observable recently when I spent some time consulting for a Fortune 500 equipment manufacturer. The marketing department had hired me to help it develop a strategy to reverse the company's declining position in one of its primary markets, oil field equipment. While the oil field equipment market had shrunk significantly in the United States, the international market remained strong. This company's international market position was being eroded, and it was not sure why. Two of the key marketing staff members were young, aggressive MBAs who had graduated from top business schools. They had each joined the company about four years earlier. Since both had analyzed the market share problem, the vice president of marketing had asked each for a written preliminary analysis that could be used to form the agenda for my discussions with the department.

The Isolating Track

One of these people, I'll call him Ted, worked very hard to isolate the primary cause behind the decline in market share. He wanted, he told me later, "to strip away all other factors, causes, and circumstances and get at the core of the problem." To do so, he had burrowed deeply into the situation, stripping away symptoms until he could confidently conclude that the decline in the market share stemmed from inadequate breadth in the product line, particularly at the low-price end. As new cost-effective methods of oil exploration and drilling had been introduced in the late 1970s and early

1980s, additional competitors had entered the market. When the price of oil declined, these new competitors remained in business by reducing prices. According to Ted's analysis, customers were moving to competitors' products because they found his own company's products too expensive. To back up his claim, he marshaled sheet after sheet of numbers, analyses, comparisons, and all sorts of quantitative evidence that clearly established the "cause of the problem." The solution? Offer lower prices and lower-end equipment alternatives to customers who would otherwise turn to competitors.

The Correlating Track

The other person, I'll call her June, displayed equal diligence in performing her analysis. Working from the opposite orientation, June had elaborately connected the declining market share with all other related factors. In order to determine whether the decline in market share stemmed from inadequate service levels, she had looked at internal issues. Did the problem relate to staffing, to morale, to the commitment of the organization, to customer satisfaction, or to other elements of the corporate culture? June also looked at the organization's overall strategy. Was the decline related to strategic positions in other markets, to industry trends or competitor strategies, to changes in customer needs, or to other external market factors? June looked at everything—from variables as specific as product delivery times to the company's overall financial position.

After completing her thorough correlative analysis, June concluded that her company's decline in market share sprang from its neglect of several underserved market segments. As the importance of international oil field markets increased, the company had neglected to recognize differences among customers, even within large oil companies. Consequently, the company had grown more and more out of touch with the unique needs and desires of different market segments. June's solution? Carefully analyze the needs of each of the underserved market segments to determine how the company could meet them. To back up her analysis, June presented clear examples of underserved customer segments her company had always perceived as mere parts of the larger market. Consequently, these customers had gone to competitors for their equipment needs because the competitors' products and services better matched their needs.

Allowing the "I" to "C"

After studying the two different presentations, I met with the marketing vice president to evaluate the respective conclusions. To his surprise, I said I found *both* analyses to be accurate. I, too, felt that the company should extend its product line, and I argued that it could better focus on underserved market segments. However, our discussion quickly turned to the outlooks of the two staff members. Given the inherent narrowness of Ted's isolating approach, its recommendation to expand the product line offered a limited solution, yet one that would certainly benefit the company. June's correlating solution, on the other hand, provided a broader solution that could potentially benefit all the company's product lines. In other words, the isolating approach solved an immediate problem, the decline in market share, while the correlating solution addressed a broader one, namely that the company did a poor job of paying attention to the needs of different market segments.

After sketching the dichotomy, I asked the marketing vice president a question: "If you could only pursue one of these courses of action, which would you choose?" He thought for a moment and then said that he would choose the correlative approach because the process of identifying and understanding the needs of underserved market segments would eventually lead to a decision to extend the product line. Pursuing just the isolating approach may solve the immediate problem, he went on, but the company might never understand exactly why it had solved the problem and how it could go on affecting the company in other ways. I agreed with him. I suggested, however, that the company needed *both* orientations. "Notice how the isolating approach brought clarity to the need for an extended product line. You need that kind of focus on short-term problem solving. But when you augment that clarity with the broader view of the correlative approach, you have the best of both worlds."

The company went on to reverse the market share decline in the specific equipment line by incorporating elements of each of the analyses. More important, it revamped its marketing analysis and strategic planning activities to emphasize a correlating orientation without dismissing the isolating orientation, which it continually used as a short-term backup to broader, longer-term analyses and plans.

10

Solutions
plus
Problems

Managers Search for Solutions; Leaders Identify Problems

Managers attack problems by immediately searching for *solutions*.
With their eyes constantly peeled for solutions, managers make
good problem solvers. In contrast, leaders worry more about *identifying* problems, anticipating all that might crop up in the future. In
a rather subtle way, managers await problems, while leaders actually go out looking for them. While managers can miss problems
because they focus so steadfastly on solutions, leaders can miss
solutions because they peer so steadily at problems on the horizon.

A good example of this difference came my way recently in the
form of a large manufacturing company run by two attorneys. Both
these men—one the CEO, the other the COO—behaved like natural leaders, constantly on the lookout for problems that might hit
their organization. In other words, they could brilliantly articulate
all the problems their company was facing or could conceivably face
in the future. Unfortunately, they were so preoccupied with identifying the problems that they neglected the solutions. While I admired their apparent holistic view of problems, I found in my consulting activities with this company that I needed to push hard for a

manager's outlook in order to counter an overemphasis on leadership at management's expense.

Problems

Paying little attention to specific solutions to specific problems, the two attorneys resorted to a single transcendent response to all problems—namely, legal action. Inevitably, they approached every problem from this angle, constantly looking for and anticipating problems and invariably relying on legal maneuvers, formal contracts, or law suits. Given their training, they felt comfortable with these solutions, which seemed to work in most instances. Since the company came under fire for alleged heavy environmental pollution, the legalistic approach often made sense, but it made less sense in other areas, especially in ongoing struggles between the management group and the board of directors. And it did not always work in such areas as pricing policies and entry into the international market. I was amazed at the virtual revolving door through which lawyers ran in and out of this company with clamoring reporters close on their heels, and I shook my head to see the company's problems constantly paraded through the press. All the legal shenanigans made tantalizing news. Of course, the company's internal culture took on an almost constant siege mentality, with people identifying every potential problem that might pop up and then moving into battle with an army of attorneys.

Solutions

Since I came aboard initially to help the company with strategic positioning and culture building, I quickly bumped up against this siege culture and its single-minded reliance on legalistic solutions. In discussions with my clients, I naturally assumed the manager's viewpoint, simply as a way to balance what I considered an overblown leader orientation. In one session with the two executives and their management team, I identified the company's current major problems and described nonlegalistic ways to attack them. Throughout, I tried to show instances where a knee-jerk legalistic response could potentially cause more problems than it would solve in the long run. As we talked about each of the major problems, I urged the group to consider solutions that did not depend on courtrooms and barristers and just might provide more long-term benefit and advantage to the corporation. Slowly, reluctantly, they began to separate certain problems from others and consider alternative solutions. With these first few faltering steps behind them, they were ready to work toward a better congruence between problems and solutions.

Congruence Between Problems and Solutions

People in the organization gradually came around to the notion that while legalistic solutions still had their place, in most cases, other types of customized solutions could bring greater and more lasting benefits. Too much reliance on legalistic solutions, born out of an overemphasis on anticipating problems and an underemphasis on developing individualized solutions, had actually jeopardized many long-term relationships and opportunities. Although the overriding legalistic solution defense had protected the company from its critics, hostile suppliers, and dissatisfied customers, it also had insulated it from potential friends and allies. In many of these instances, nonlegalistic problem solving could win more friends and influence more people than lawsuits ever could. Clearly, improved strategic alliances and partnerships would benefit the organization in the long term.

In the end, the company's executives agreed in principle to practice more tailored problem solving. To do this, they thought deeply about the congruence between a problem and a solution, placing legal action where it belonged, as a last resort. They started using more consultants with nonlegalistic backgrounds, and they hired two senior-level professional managers to oversee corporate staff functions. Only a few months later, the company did, in fact, enter into an attractive strategic partnership with the local community. Yes, the partnership included a lot of legal maneuvering. However, the legal maneuvering and contracts reflected a spirit of cooperation rather than the old spirit of combat. The company would not have come up with this solution had it remained true to its former problem-solving style.

Leaders may be brilliant at identifying problems, and managers may be adept at finding solutions to particular problems, but neither can survive alone. The balanced and integrated company does both.

11

Markets
plus
Customers

Managers Service Markets; Leaders Serve Customers

Most managers focus on the collective groups of customers that make up a *market*, thereby adopting a relatively impersonal attitude toward the marketplace. As with many other aspects of business, the manager's mind thinks about markets in fairly analytical and quantitative terms, and is comfortable with such terms as *market share*, *market penetration*, *market segments*, *market growth*, *market life cycle*, and so on. This often results in a somewhat detached outlook.

The leader, in contrast, prefers a much more qualitative and human view of the marketplace and likes to think of a market in terms of individual *customers*. The leader's soul takes into account the human side of customers — the feelings, emotions, needs, and wants that cause customers to purchase a product or service. Concerned about trends in these areas as well as buying preferences and sociological, demographic, and economic shifts among customers, the leader's strategic outlook tends toward the personal and subjective. When formulating competitive strategy, both outlooks are extremely important, even though they often produce quite different outcomes.

A few years ago, a large electric utility taught me again about this difference between market and customer orientation. I had been hired by the company to aid them with some extensive strategic and organizational work it had undertaken. Like many large corporations, this utility had institutionalized a bureaucracy that looked at and thought about markets in certain ways. Assuming that it had clearly identified and analyzed its market, the utility had set rates to meet the needs of particular market segments. Its highly analytical and statistical approach led to an impersonal, detached, and aloof attitude toward the company's customers. As I dug into the utility's history and environment, I soon discovered that while its monopolistic position had fueled its detached approach to its markets, other factors contributed to it as well — chiefly the fact that died-in-the-wool managers ran the show.

The Down Side of Market Orientation

During the late 1970s and early 1980s, increased competition in the electric utility industry forced this particular utility to face some very tough issues, such as the fact that it had never felt a need to behave in a truly customer-responsive manner. While the company had developed sophisticated analytical marketing and rate-setting capabilities, it had become so distant from the actual customers using its power that it could no longer recognize, much less address, real customer needs. While the company's top executives could tell you all about usage patterns and the quantitative aspects of each market segment and rate schedule, they didn't really understand the power needs and desires of their customers. As municipal governments in their territory sought to generate and distribute their own power, this problem became more and more acute. Large industrial customers also found ways to enter into cogeneration joint ventures with other utilities to generate and distribute their own electrical power. All this came as a tremendous shock to the once-dominant utility. How in the world could it get back in touch with its customers?

The Up Side of Customer Orientation

In the course of my consultation with this utility, a new president came aboard, and as I had hoped, Wilson Gates (not his real name) was a leader with a new kind of vision for the company's future. Having participated in recommending Gates for the presidency precisely for his customer orientation, I was pleased to see him live up to his advanced billing. He launched the utility into a new relationship with the marketplace characterized by the motto "We Want To Be Our Customer's Choice." This motto sent a clear message to its customers. Proclaiming it, Gates engineered an intensive campaign to get in touch with customers throughout the utility's distribution system and thereby to understand their needs and wants before initiating any new programs.

Before long, the company began offering its own cogeneration services to large industrial customers, began providing free energy audits to its residential customers, and introduced a host of joint-venture options for corporations and government entities alike. The shift from market to customer orientation was not easy for many in the company because it required a totally different mind set, not to mention hands-on involvement with customers as people. Still, it gradually became evident, even to some people in the quantitatively oriented rate and marketing departments, that a long history of market orientation had really shortchanged the customer, and as the months went by, more and more people within the utility grudgingly came to appreciate the value of the new approach.

Customers Comprise the Basic Unit of Markets

Before I tell you what happened in this particular situation, I'd like to describe my own view of the ideal relationship between market and customer viewpoints. Because the customer comprises the basic unit of any market or market segment, a company must always place its primary emphasis on the customer. Otherwise, a company can easily fall into the trap of misunderstanding, misreading, or neglecting the genuine needs and wants of very human customers. While the market view does offer a valuable and necessary tool, it often fails to treat customers as individuals. Without first focusing on the individual, you cannot develop a truly appropriate, accurate, and meaningful view of the collection of people who form the over-all market. In this particular case, then, the leader's view should probably come first. Once it takes hold, then managers can freely develop a necessary market orientation.

Sadly, my utility company client could not handle the massive changes Wilson Gates introduced. Day in and day out, he spent virtu-ally all his time struggling to get his executives and employees to feel the need for change and believe in the viability of the proposed course of action. As happened in other utilities during this trying period for the industry, Gates eventually resigned in frustration, worked as a consultant for two years, and then came back as chairman of the board. When he returned, the company's attitude had finally changed suffi-ciently to afford clear recognition throughout of the vision it had so strongly resisted earlier. Now people much more eagerly accepted the need for change. Today the utility industry ranks this company as one of the most innovative in the country, especially in terms of cus-tomer responsiveness. Financially, it performs more solidly than it did ten years ago and has become a sort of model for the future, when customers seeking electrical power will be able to choose among more and more alternatives.

12

Rivals
plus
Partners

Managers Think Rivals; Leaders Seek Partners

Whereas managers approach the world in a competitive stance, leaders see that same world full of potential partners. The manager's mind tends to think in terms of competitive market warfare; the leader's soul seeks an alternative to market warfare that doesn't remove competition but actually improves it through mutually beneficial and legal arrangements or partnerships. As the world becomes more and more of a global marketplace and competition grows even more fierce, managers will probably feel it even more imperative to position themselves in relationship to perceived *rivals*. Leaders, on the other hand, will probably try even harder to forge strategic *partnerships* with others.

In the next decade, competitiveness will most likely become more critical to success than ever. Yet at the same time, companies will find traditional routes to obtaining and sustaining competitive advantages more crowded and less fruitful. They will need to find new and different, even unorthodox, ways to turn would-be rivals into eager partners. Leaders will push for new forms of partnerships and strategic alliances, managers will prefer competition, pure and simple.

In my own recent experience, the Europeans seem to be lead-ing in this regard, with the Americans continuing to manage by comparison. This came home to me when I did some work for a Scandinavian manufacturing and distribution firm. As this com-pany wrestled with the reality of global competition and the prob-ability of intensified local and regional competition stimulated by a more open European economic community, its management con-cluded that its success depended on finding other ways to compete besides hand-to-hand combat.

Old Style Competition

During the early 1980s, SVS, as I will refer to it, had tried to impress upon its world of customers that it offered total solutions to indus-trial equipment and supply problems. Assuming that if it did not provide a full range of products and services it would lose business to competitors, SVS had formed arrangements with a multitude of suppliers for the primary purpose of providing one-stop shopping for its customers. In this way, SVS could offer everything from fork-lifts to cleaning solutions. Of course, its success soon prompted competitors to start playing the same game, and before long, several industrial equipment and products firms were attempting to pro-vide total solutions and a full range of products and services. Hand-to-hand combat broke out all up and down the line. It didn't take long, however, for the managing director of SVS to realize that this rivalistic approach was getting his company nowhere. Trained as a manager, he felt reluctant to try something different, but the leader in him overcame this reluctance.

New Style Competition

Recognizing that when it comes to combat, even winners carry away some scars, the managing director initiated discussions with two of his major competitors in the hope of finding even better ways to offer customers total solutions, but now through a strategic alliance that would allow one competitor to provide one set of products and services and another competitor to offer another set. Stopping short of a merger, these three competitors coordinated their efforts by first focusing on different product groupings and then by banding together to offer the full range of products or the total solution their customers might want. In this way, each competitor could narrow its focus, increase its value, and become better at satisfying customer needs, more efficient at delivering products and services, and more adept at forming loyal bonds with suppliers. In theory, the customer would win, each competitor would win, and the industry as a whole would win. One plus one equals three.

Despite some early resistance from his former rivals, this managing director's vision took hold and became a reality. With the end results proving far better than even he had imagined early on, he is now looking for more opportunities to do the same thing in other areas. Never has the well-being, viability, and profitability of his firm looked healthier.

The Tempered Perspective

Although companies do set up similar alliances in the United States today, they usually do so via merger or acquisition, tactics that quickly reach a limit in a particular industry or market. To compete abroad, U.S. business, with the help of government, must find ways to forge more creative strategic partnerships in the future.

Given the nature of the American free enterprise system, we must be careful to avoid either extreme of competition. Focusing only on rivalries and the existing rules of competition may seriously prevent our organizations from finding creative solutions to the problems of intensified global competition. By the same token, certain strategic alliances and partnerships violate existing laws and can get you thrown in jail or slapped with a major antitrust suit. Thus we must adopt a tempered perspective, balancing the impulses of our managers and leaders. The proper proportion of each will depend on the circumstances.

In Europe, you may be able to act more as a leader, while in the United States, especially in consolidated industries that can sustain no more mergers and acquisitions, you may have to play more of a manager. However, while certain forms of cooperation may be easier to accomplish in Europe than in the United States, cooperation is becoming more and more viable and possible everywhere. Only recently the U.S. high-tech industry has created research and manufacturing consortiums that may pave the way here and elsewhere for more creative and valuable solutions to the problems of competition and cooperation.

13

Incremental
plus
Sweeping

Managers Design Incremental Strategies;
Leaders Lay Out Sweeping Strategies

In most cases, managers will break strategies into a series of small, *incremental* gains. This reflects managers' preferences for getting things done in an orderly, logical fashion, putting one foot in front of the other to avoid tripping over or getting ahead of themselves. Consequently, managers usually look for the small opportunities to strengthen market position, improve services, enhance quality, provide better customer responsiveness, and so on. A series of small wins, they believe, will add up to a major and sustainable victory in the marketplace. Leaders, more geared toward breakthrough opportunities, prefer to assemble *sweeping* strategies that can produce dramatic results. They want big wins.

In essence, managers design what McKinsey & Company calls *same-game strategies*, (i.e., strategic positioning that does not alter the basic nature of the game being played in the marketplace), while leaders lay out what McKinsey & Company calls *new-game strategies* (i.e., strategies that create new businesses, redefine markets, and seek unprecedented advantages).

One company followed the incremental approach, growing slowly but steadily over a number of years. However, when this communications firm, I'll refer to it as World Comm, found itself in a rapidly changing industry and market with newly aggressive competitors it decided that the time had come for it to consider a more dramatic approach to strategic positioning. In other words, external forces were pushing it from a management to a leadership posture. Many companies wilt under such pressure, but this one did surprisingly well.

The Incremental Past

In existence for about ten years, World Comm had grown consistently by selling a variety of communications products and services (i.e., telephones, radio systems, satellites, satellite link-up service, and custom-designed production studios and broadcast communications vans) primarily to a single region of the country, but also to an international market in some cases. As competition heated up and technological changes accelerated within the industry, World Comm decided that it should try to transcend its limited position. Most of the company's past strategic planning had focused on improving its product lines, acquiring better ones, upgrading its service, slowly expanding its sales territories, and generally looking for small, incremental wins in the marketplace. By doing so, it established a reputation for stability and even stodginess. The banks loved the company, but banks tend to love the past more than the future. World Comm's executives now felt that while the incremental strategy approach had worked in the past, it probably couldn't sustain the future. This is where I came into the picture — to help this company consider more sweeping strategies.

The Sweeping Future

As the firm's executive committee began searching for new strategic alternatives that would dramatically position the company in its rapidly changing industry, it needed to decide which new devices and products to manufacture and which to distribute. The first step was to draw an accurate map of how the industry was changing and what those changes meant to the future of the company. Then the executive committee began considering new-game strategies, such as focusing only on becoming the premier broadcast communications van producer in the world or becoming a top-flight mobile telephone and radio communications specialist. Such new-game strategies could and would redefine the whole industry.

Of course, the management group, steeped in incremental strategic thinking, found this exercise both difficult and frustrating. After much resistance and discussion, however, the group finally began to gravitate toward a strategy that would convert the firm into a multilevel sales organization. When the idea first came up, it alarmed the executive group, but as the group debated the idea, it came to understand and appreciate how powerfully the idea could influence the company's future. No one else in the industry was employing this strategy, and it did offer clear opportunities for building on the firm's already successful sales function. The strategy would focus primarily on standard, noncustomized communication products such as telephones and radios, selling them through regional, national, and then international sales organizations. The company would put into place the multilevel sales principles practiced by such companies as Amway.

Incremental Today, Sweeping Tomorrow

Strategically, the best organizations gracefully blend incremental with dramatic strategies as circumstances dictate. Such organizations know when and how to manage and lead. Without the ability to do both, companies in the future will find themselves slipping further behind more nimble competitors. In the case of World Comm, nimbleness paid off. After a year of operating with a multilevel sales force, World Comm had surpassed the volume of sales previously generated with traditional approaches. Sales had increased by one-third and would increase by another third in the coming year. Now the company blended in the incremental mode, building on its sweeping new strategy in a step-by-step way. After separating off the satellite and customized products and services side of the business, the executive committee used its new-found strategic flexibility to inaugurate new-game strategies for these businesses, while continuing with incremental strategies in the telephone and radio businesses.

Had the president of World Comm not recognized and acted on the need to move in new directions, his managers would have kept plodding along the incremental path. In my experience, few presidents find it easy to nimbly blend management and leadership orientations. Many executives can't do it at all. Those who can usually work for balanced and integrated organizations that can tap the natural tension between managers and leaders. Without maintaining positive tension on a continuing basis, an organization either never effectively employs both incremental and sweeping strategies, or it does so only as a desperate gamble.

14

Weaknesses plus Strengths

Managers Correct Strategic Weaknesses; Leaders Build on Strategic Strengths

When it comes to looking at strategic direction, strategic advantage, and strategic positioning, managers first tend to look at the firm's *weaknesses* in relation to competitors, assuming that by doing so they can strengthen any areas of deficiency and thus improve their strategic and competitive position. As much as they may talk about strategic strengths, managers concentrate most heavily on correcting weaknesses because they worry that weaknesses can drag down or neutralize strengths. The manager's mind thinks more about factors that can prevent strategic success than about factors that will enhance it.

Leaders, on the other hand, approach strategic positioning from the standpoint of *strengths*, identifying and building on what the firm does well. Working from strengths, leaders assume, will raise the whole operation to a higher level of performance because one strong area in an organization can eventually boost all other areas.

Recently I worked with a rapidly growing high-technology

firm run by a group of managers and leaders who prided themselves on understanding the very latest in management thought
and practice. Everyone in this group was highly educated, hard-
driving, and determined to make the company one of the best-run
companies in the world. The company manufactured and marketed
high-powered personal computers and engineering workstations,
with a strong emphasis on workstation networking.

Having just concluded several months of strategic analysis and
planning with the aid of two major consulting firms, the company
asked me to help resolve a thorny issue that had sprung up. While
one of the consulting firms had focused on the company's strengths
as the basis for developing a long-term strategic direction, the other
had developed an alternative approach that highlighted weaknesses and potential failing points that could prevent the organization from achieving its goals. One approach represented a success-
enhancement mode; the other, a failure-avoidance one. In fact, the
company was so cash rich that strategic thinking and analysis had
become somewhat of a game for the management group, which
explained why the group had engaged two consulting firms with
diametrically opposed approaches. Once both consulting groups
had completed their analyses, I came in to attend a day-long
decision-making session at which the management team planned
to dissect both approaches and then take the best of each.

Weak Points

The consulting firm that had touched on weak points and drawn up
failing scenarios had identified plenty of areas that could, unat-
tended, pose potential threats to the firm. Correcting these would
presumably avoid failure and thus guarantee success. To make a
long story short, the weakness-oriented process concluded that this
high-tech company would face its greatest threats in the area of
production. Yes, it should shore up several other areas that could
cause damage over the long haul, but production could be a real
killer. The analysis concluded that careful management of the firm's
production capabilities could ensure growth and profit goals, retain

customers by not overpromising, and protect financial resources by avoiding overproduction. In short, the production function within the company provided the key to avoiding failure and gaining success and should therefore serve as the focal point for strategic planning. Production scheduling, production facilities planning, production quality, and production output were the key strategic variables.

Strong Points

The more traditional analysis by the other consultants stressed strengths, arguing that these, not weaknesses, should inform the company's strategic direction and priorities. This approach implied that a well-run company builds on strengths because, after all, its strengths got it to where it is today. Not surprisingly, this analysis concluded that the company should devote most of its attention to product innovation and development, two areas that largely accounted for its current success. Although the report cited other strengths, it relied heavily on the argument that if the company lost its edge in product innovation, no amount of strength in other areas could compensate for that loss. In short, product innovation provided the key to gaining more and more success, and therefore, it should serve as the focal point of strategic planning. Product ideas, product concepts, product characteristics, product design, and product performance were the key strategic variables.

Strong Points plus Weak Points

When the day-long meeting began, the major questions on everyone's mind were: Where should we place our focus, on maintaining and enhancing our ability to innovate and develop product or on strengthening our production capability? Can we do both? Should we do both? What will happen if we emphasize one area over the other? These and similar questions formed the heart of the day's agenda.

Opposing factions quickly formed. One outspoken manager, I'll call him Monroe, believed that to succeed in the future, the company must do a good job in both innovation and production. However, he proposed that the company should primarily work on production in the short term because that area needed the most help. Another voice in the group, I'll refer to him as Staples, proposed a different scenario, which argued that the company should further strengthen innovation because that area demands the constant attention of any world-class high-technology product development firm. In other words, put the production cart behind the horse of innovation, not vice versa.

As we came to the end of our day together, the Monroe and Staples factions had each stated their cases quite eloquently, but as we tried to hammer out a consensus, we reached an impasse. One plus one did not work: The horse and the cart couldn't stand in front of each other at the same time.

At this point, representatives from each of the two consulting firms rose to offer final comments about their respective strategies. Listening to them, I recalled all those intellectual debates in graduate school where we forever argued the appropriateness of different strategic decisions. When the group asked me for my observations on the day's discussions and the months of strategic analysis that had proceeded them, I suggested that the most successful companies in the future would be those which could do many things well. I indicated that this would be especially true for the computer industry in general and in the workstation networking and linking arena in particular. From the looks on their faces, Monroe's contingent seemed to sense victory in the wings.

However, I quickly pointed out that the path to high levels of performance in many areas would probably come from stressing strengths before weaknesses. In my experience, the firms that continued to enhance and build on their key strengths set the right tone for all areas in their organizations. Now the Staples group sensed victory.

However, I went on, great companies never take a narrow and myopic approach, focusing only on one strength, but rather they adopt the wider view, stressing the ultimate need to be strong in multiple areas. Thus analysis of weaknesses does make sense, in the right proportion. Finally, I suggested that the company watch the production area carefully and put it on a long-term development track that would eventually strengthen it to the point where it could shine as brightly as innovation and product development.

The day concluded, and in the ensuing months the company did, in fact, continue to focus on its primary strength, maintaining its position as a major innovator in the high-powered personal computer and engineering workstation markets. At the same time, production management gradually improved, until the cart and the horse began to enjoy fairly equal status as company strengths. The moral of the story: Building on strengths plus shoring up weaknesses does equal superior performance, but only if both are pursued in tandem. Building on strengths should never justify neglecting weaknesses, and shoring up weaknesses should never mean de-emphasizing strengths.

III

Organizational Culture/ Capability

Interest in organizational cultures and capabilities blossomed in the mid-1980s after many business writers, thinkers, and executives began emphasizing anew the human side of enterprise. Under various labels, organizational culture has always concerned the best companies, and while we have come to explain and talk about it a lot in recent years, organizational culture always has played and will continue to play a major role in shaping the responsiveness, quality, problem-solving ability, and distinctive competence of every organization in the private or public sectors. As in the case of the other success factors, managers and leaders approach organizational cultures and capabilities very differently, with management-dominated organizations tending to perpetuate existing organizational cultures and capabilities and leadership-driven organizations tending to create new cultures and capabilities. Conflict-oriented organizations create environments that provoke constant change in cultures and capabilities with the ebb and flow of the confrontation.

In the vacillation-prone organization, organizational cultures and capabilities often become confused, moving up and down and back and forth, never revealing which values and philosophies to embrace. Only in the balanced and integrated organization does the natural tension between managers and leaders help renew organizational cultures and capabilities. Renewal springs from a deep valuing and blending of all the many different management and leadership traits.

In this section we'll explore a number of organizational culture and capability issues within the context of management and leadership. In each case you will see different ways in which management plus leadership can continually renew and revitalize organizational cultures and capabilities.

15

Authority plus Influence

Managers Wield Authority; Leaders Apply Influence

Authority gives someone the power to command behavior. Managers wield it to get people to take action. Without authority, managers feel powerless and frustrated. In contrast, *influence* involves the use of indirect or less tangible means to prompt thought and opinion, as well as behavior. Leaders apply influence rather than authority to get people to take action. Unlike managers, leaders do not feel uncomfortable in situations with unclear lines of authority. Authority and influence differ in much the same way that a hard sell differs from a soft sell. One is forceful and direct; the other is more subtle and indirect.

A decade ago I became deeply involved in a gubernatorial race that allowed me to observe a classic distinction between authority and influence. The incumbent Democratic governor, an attorney with an uncanny ability to rally opinion leaders throughout the state behind statewide concerns, enjoyed tremendous popularity among the Republican majority in the state. The challenger was a very different sort of fellow, who, since he had his work cut out defeating the incumbent, hired me and others to help him. Beginning the task with a detailed study of our rival's record, I soon determined that his "hands-off" approach, while politically effective, had placed state government operations on the brink of a potential downhill slide. Thus I targeted unmasking the financial and management problems in the state government as our campaign's major focus. To our astonishment, few people accepted our analysis at first. It turned out that the incumbent's style misleadingly communicated competent leadership. I felt strongly that while the incumbent certainly could influence opinion leaders and citizens' groups throughout the state, especially when confronting highly visible issues, his influence could not replace authoritative action when it actually came to operating the state's bureaucracy.

Style Without Substance

As we got the challenger's campaign underway, the incumbent's vulnerability became more and more apparent. However, the incumbent's masterful image manipulation kept his influence strong as he obtained federal funds to address a critical water problem, protected vital natural resources, attracted new business, and launched a campaign dubbed "Agenda for the Eighties." All this stylish image building gave people the impression of a brilliant leader paving the way into a bright future.

Against the veneer of the governor's style, the challenger could not easily convey the substantive issue of mismanagement. Despite growing evidence of the costly consequences of allowing state agencies to run themselves with little or no direction from the governor, and despite perilously low state revenues and an anticipated drop in the state's bond rating from AAA to A, the challenger's attack made little headway.

The incumbent stepped up his stylish campaign tactics, using his influence to communicate a feeling of well-being and hope for the state and maintained an astonishing 76 percent public approval rating.

Substance Without Style

For his part, the challenger, also a highly competent attorney, had gained substantial experience in the public sector, where he had demonstrated unquestioned skill as an effective manager who was able to ferret out and solve sticky problems. Convinced of the incumbent's mismanagement, the challenger raised the issue every time he spoke during the last three months of the campaign. Unfortunately, the challenger lacked the influence it takes to sway group thoughts or feelings. Having always relied heavily on authority to get things done, he fell short when it came to rallying others behind a vision or purpose. Even in the three debates between the two, the challenger could not make his charges stick because the incumbent succeeded in dispelling all doubts with brilliant flashes of style.

Finally, in the last month of the campaign, the state auditor and the state attorney general agreed to go on camera with their own "authority-backed" views of state government mismanagement. When the resultant television spot created the anticipated stir of attention, with television stations assigning investigative teams to the issue, the challenger began to attract a more receptive audience. Still, even though polls started shifting in the final days of the campaign, it turned out to be too little, too late. The incumbent won reelection.

Substance with Style

The moral of this story is not that the wrong man won, but that neither possessed nor orchestrated all the qualities and characteristics needed to run the state effectively. The incumbent was a master of influence; the challenger, a master of authority. Neither knew when and how to blend the two into an ideal combination. When influence becomes a person's singular focus, it often creates a vacuum behind it that makes detailed implementation difficult, particularly when no backup authority exists. By the same token, when authority is the only focus, it usually fails to rally the troops, employees, or citizens with the kind of motivation it takes to move them forward in the first place. One does work without the other, but not as well as both together.

In the end, the governor made some attempts to rectify the state's management problems by removing the director of finance and a few other key administrators. Things didn't really change, however, because the reelected governor, not truly believing he needed to change his ways, continued applying influence without wielding authority.

Four years later, faced with an uphill battle, the incumbent governor shrewdly chose not to run again. Although the challenger threw his hat in the ring once again, he failed to win his party's nomination because he could not sufficiently influence his party's leaders and delegates to rally behind his leadership.

These two politicians would have made a brilliant team. Every state (not to mention every public or private organization) desperately needs leaders with strong influence and managers who use authority to get things done. Balanced attention to both allows an organization to focus on the key issues facing it, as well as on the nuts and bolts of daily operation.

16

Uniformity plus Unity

Managers Seek Uniformity; Leaders Pursue Unity

Managers, who by nature prefer a stable, orderly environment, feel most secure when their organizations attain a degree of *uniformity*. To their minds, uniformity, which suggests a rather well-oiled machine that hums along in a consistent, systematic, and predictable fashion, creates a more easily managed environment. In the uniform organization, the manager can measure, compare, and correct situations with an engineering mentality.

The leader, on the other hand, could care less about uniformity or orderliness, as long as everyone in the organization unites behind a common purpose, principle, idea, or vision. *Unity* of heart and mind, not managerial uniformity of actions or practices, preoccupies the leader. With the manager arguing that uniformity breeds unity, the leader counters that uniformity does nothing to promote common resolve or intent which builds unity.

A successful chain of superstores selling office products struggled long and hard with this very issue. This company had grown from start-up to over $600 million in revenues in only five years.

Catering primarily to small businesses, but open to general membership at slightly higher prices, this company developed an approach to merchandise selection and presentation that became a model for the industry. Charles, the chief financial officer, and Dean, the vice president of operations (not their real names), held opposing views on the uniformity-versus-unity issue. Charles worked diligently to establish uniformity throughout the company, especially in the area of financial policies and procedures. In contrast, Dean worked equally hard to get each store to respond to the unique needs of its customers by building a shared vision among store managers and employees to meet the needs of the local customer, no matter what. As you might guess, these two executives clashed on principles from time to time, but they usually resolved their differences more or less amicably. However, after a period of rapid expansion, during which the company opened twenty new stores, Charles chafed over an increasing disregard for standard operating procedures, while Dean congratulated himself that local operations were finally achieving the kind of autonomy and flexibility he felt they needed.

In a subsequent staff meeting, the inevitable donnybrook occurred. When Charles bitterly accused Dean of flagrant disregard for current operating standards, Dean accused Charles of forgetting how the company made money in the first place. The president of the company, I'll call him Wallace, knowing the two men's ingrained preferences and viewpoints, refereed the bout by trying to get them both to put themselves in the other guy's shoes.

Marching in Step to an Out-of-Tune Band

Although a high level of uniformity can signify a high level of unity, uniformity often provides only an illusion of unity, masking low levels of commitment, poor morale, and indifference toward corporate goals. Organizational uniformity, which relates to actions and practices rather than to hearts and minds, simply signals that people have learned to behave in similar ways. If pursued in the extreme, organizational uniformity can severely constrain and compromise creativity, individuality, fulfillment, and genuine unity. To better illustrate the difference, Wallace talked about the Stanford marching band: "Perhaps you've seen their half-time antics: a rag-tag army of musicians, many dressed in outrageous costumes, storming onto the field in disarray. But then they suddenly form a neat pattern, and when they start playing their instruments, they make beautiful music. They lack uniformity, but they sure have unity. In contrast, picture a band with spiffy, identical uniforms marching lock-step onto the field, who, when they start playing their instruments, sound like a cat fight on a hot-tin roof. Lots of uniformity, no unity."

In the case of the chain of superstores, unity of purpose and vision, in terms of meeting customer needs, was certainly a central issue. The company's profitability and market share largely depended on unity among managers and employees (whom the company calls associates) behind the "local needs" principle, which led some stores to stock unique new merchandise, fulfill special orders, make unusual deliveries, receive returned merchandise against customary policy, and adapt credit policies to customers with oddball credit backgrounds. Whenever managers and employees at a given store did not unite behind the principle, that store usually turned in a lackluster long-term performance compared to others. After stressing this fact to Charles, Wallace asked him point blank whether or not he'd put taking care of a customer ahead of a uniform procedure or standard? Before Wallace permitted an answer, however, he turned to Dean.

Dancing Fast to a Slow Waltz

When organizations gather momentum behind a united purpose, principle, idea, or goal, not much can stop them. However, when such an organization fails to back up its unity with appropriate operating practices, procedures, and standards, it can court disaster. It happens all the time, because an organization good at forging unity usually fosters a lot of diversity among its people, saying in effect, "As long as you remain faithful to our vision, we don't care how you *act* to fulfill that vision." Of course, this is fine to a point.

Once the superstores achieved collective resolve among its people to go out of their way to meet customer needs, it naturally emphasized flexibility and autonomy in decision making at the local level. In this context, people will understandably resist uniform standards or procedures, even those critical to the company's financial stability. For example, ignoring operating standards for how to handle cash at a store location may lead to conscious or unconscious abuse by employees. Disregarding creditworthiness standards in order to meet a customer's needs may lead to unnecessary and avoidable losses. Again, Wallace used a music analogy: "Let's say we've got the band all tuned up, only this time it's a dance band. I know people do their own thing to rock and roll, but suppose the band plays a waltz. Wouldn't you look silly doing the twist to "Two Hearts in Three Quarter Time"? You sure wouldn't win any dance contests." He then asked Dean, "When would you ignore uniform operating standards or procedures in the name of building unity behind a worthy purpose?" Before letting him answer this question, Wallace encouraged each man to defend the other's position. "Perhaps," he said, "you might discover some common ground."

Uniformity that Supports Rather than Destroys Unity

This exercise in debate did help Charles and Dean appreciate each other's ideas and jobs more deeply. In the end, they did find some common ground that represented not so much a compromise as a synthesis of viewpoints. They articulated it this way: "Standards should always be challenged, but never ignored."

Think about this statement. It implies that standards are important, but also that they should not be set in concrete. It allows for marching in step to the drum, but it also permits different drummers and new dances whenever they become necessary. Such an approach would serve to help new stores and employees focus on building unity of purpose and resolve, but it also would avoid wasting time and resources reinventing workable operating standards and procedures. In the case of the chain of superstores, changes in standards would require the approval of the executive committee, which the president guaranteed would happen swiftly.

At the end of the staff meeting, two formerly feuding executives realized that neither one believed in the indiscriminate violation of necessary standards or in the unnecessary compromising of the united resolve to move all obstacles to the fulfillment of a customer's needs. In my own experience, unconstrained uniformity can limit and even destroy real unity of purpose. At the same time, recklessly ignoring the need for uniformity in the pursuit of unity will eventually threaten the viability and the unity of the organization.

17

Programs
plus
People

Managers Administer Programs; Leaders Watch People

The manager concentrates on *implementing programs* to get things done more than the leader does. The leader prefers to concentrate on *people* and their progress within the organization. While the manager designs a program suitable for all, the leader worries about how each individual will feel about and adapt to the priorities, goals, and purposes of the organization and whether the organization indeed fulfills each individual performing tasks within it. Managers use programs to move people; leaders move people to use programs.

Consider this hypothetical example. When a "garden variety" problem crops up, the manager will often fall back on a program to solve it. Take, for instance, the manager who implements a time-card program to solve a tardiness problem among the clerical staff. Everyone ends up under the program, possibly even people in other departments with no record of tardiness. In contrast, the leader would pursue a very different course of action, working through people to identify the exact causes of the tardiness problem. The leader's solution would most likely apply to that cause and not necessarily influence everyone in the organization.

Recently, I became involved with a major commercial lending bank with over a hundred branches scattered throughout a large region of the country. Over the last several years, as with most banks, the organization has been going through a major transition from traditional finance-oriented banking services to a more customer service, market-oriented posture. Obviously, the shift demanded a major alteration of the corporate culture. The president of the bank, Alex Randall (not his real name), was a leader who had built the organization to its current size over the past twenty years primarily through close attention to people management. A master at solving people puzzles, Randall had nurtured many strong officers and branch managers throughout the system.

In the midst of the current change process, Randall hired a vice president of marketing, Myrna Milani (not her real name), who turned out to be a manager accustomed to relying on programs to bring about change. Milani had come from another financial services organization where programs ruled the day. There were programs for employee training, programs for customer service, programs for how to dress, programs for performance improvement, programs for conducting customer questionnaires, and on and on. Almost everything in her previous environment had been programmed, and her former firm enjoyed above-average levels of success. During the first year in her new position, Milani implemented a total of eleven new programs designed to help branch managers and commercial lending officers become more marketing-oriented and customer-driven.

About this time I began consulting with Alex Randall, who asked me to assess the culture-change process. Concerned that Milani's programs had not brought about the desired results and had actually "turned off" many branch managers and loan officers throughout the banking system, Randall wanted an objective appraisal of exactly why the programs hadn't worked and what should be done now and in the future. After some preliminary analysis, I submitted my report.

Working Through Programs

I began by recapping the bank's cultural history, detailing how, over the past twenty years, Randall had succeeded in developing a group of competent managers committed to the bank's future. During that twenty-year period, few bankwide programs had come into play. Of course, people followed certain standard operating procedures. But when it came to management and providing services to customers, each branch had enjoyed great freedom in creating its own operating philosophy and carving its niche in the marketplace. Because Randall had so carefully groomed his managers, he also could trust them completely, giving them a great deal of autonomy to run their branches as they saw fit. This style of operation had clearly worked for many years.

Now new pressures on the bank from competitors, customers, and a general revolution in the financial services industry were requiring this bank to be more sensitive to marketing and customer service issues. Instead of responding to these pressures in the traditional people-oriented way, Randall had hired a program-oriented vice president who believed that change would come about only by means of new programs.

The branch managers and commercial lending officers were totally unprepared for such a departure from the people-oriented, high-trust, high-autonomy style that had governed the past twenty years. Now, in the course of only one year, they had seen eleven new systemwide programs imposed, and they were reeling. Most resisted the programs because they signaled a lack of trust, not to mention a reduction in autonomy. One program Milani had designed to improve customer relations required branch managers and loan officers to fill out a customer profile for every customer, and then apply the information to a strategic selling matrix to determine what additional products or services the bank could offer that customer. This departed radically from the warm, informal relationships that branch managers and loan officers had been encouraged to develop with customers over the years, which had always resulted in a deeper understanding of customer needs plus better service and additional business for the bank. With this new program, the managers and loan officers felt like they were artificially manipulating their customers, a feeling they didn't like at all. Over the months, many bank managers subconsciously rebelled against and even subverted the programs. Although some of the managers had tried to communicate their feelings and concerns to Randall, he had dismissed the feedback as resistance to change and a natural impulse to cling to the past. He himself had believed that major change required major new programs.

Working Through People

Describing the natural tension between the programs and people side of change efforts, I suggested to Randall that he should have been utilizing his old tried and proven management style because it had worked so well in the past. A culture based on working through people, I pointed out, would react most favorably to the same approach, no matter how much change it needed to make. Why had he decided that working through people and allowing key people to run parts of the organization and develop their own programs wouldn't work as well today as it had yesterday? I then helped him understand that the current widespread frustration in his organization had come about mainly as a result of the very basic difference between his leadership style and that of his new marketing vice president. Milani wasn't incompetent, of course. Her approach simply ran counter to the culture's experience.

How Programs and People Can Work Together

Without question, organizations need programs to implement change and to achieve desired results. However, successful programs depend on people getting behind them. All I did in this case was provide the president with needed reassurance that he should continue to focus on people first and programs second. Once he regained confidence in his leadership style, things turned around quickly. Where formerly he had begun to appear hesitant and confused about the future, he now appeared excited and determined.

As I continued to work with the bank, the people/programs issue arose often enough to cause some people to wonder whether Randall shouldn't just go ahead and fire Milani. Strongly disagreeing with that sentiment, I urged him to work with her to find ways in which she could subordinate her programs to a wider people focus. In other words, how could the bank implement necessary programs without subverting the autonomy and decision-making ability of branch presidents and commercial loan officers?

The answer lay in placing Milani's ability to develop and implement new programs at the disposal of all the branch presidents, managers, and commercial lending officers throughout the banking system. Thus she could help the branches tailor programs to meet their particular needs and those of their customers. In no way would this erode Randall's commitment to managing through people first. While the bank would never become as program-oriented as Milani's former environment, it could benefit from the introduction of programs at the branch level that did not compromise an overall people orientation. And, when key programs worked well in one branch they could be more readily introduced and adapted to the other branches because the branch presidents and loan officers wanted them.

In conclusion, people should precede programs, *never* vice versa. Leaders must blend their efforts with managers to ensure that people receive greater attention and a higher priority than programs. Then, appropriate programs can come in due course — and into a welcoming, rather than a resistant, environment.

18

Policy
plus
Example

Managers Formulate Policies; Leaders Set Examples

Managers use *policies* to enforce their management. By *policies*, I mean procedures, programs, mechanisms, systems, and processes that set forth a series of rules and regulations, be they formal or informal. Interestingly, the words "policy" and "police" share the same root. Without *policing*, contends the manager, an organization would fall apart, its people growing confused and moving off in different directions. The mind of the manager holds that one obtains acceptable behavior by getting people to follow established policies that clearly specify that behavior.

Leaders, however, rely on their own personal *example* to influence people. They believe that a good example provides a far more powerful motivational device than all the rules and regulations in the world. This doesn't mean that leaders disdain policies altogether, it simply means that leaders pay less attention to them. Likewise, this doesn't mean managers are not examples of desired behavior; they simply rely more heavily on policies to bring about desired behavior. Under a strong leader, other individuals in an organization begin to set similar examples themselves and thus

become additional models of desired behavior. Of course, this notion of modeling acceptable behavior often comes unconsciously
from the leader's soul.

With respect to this divergence between policy and example, I
once found myself in a sticky situation with a federal government
agency. A division head, I'll call him Reynolds, had asked me to
come in and take a look at some of the things he was trying to do to
improve the workings of his agency. Although he impressed me as
a good leader with a noble quest, I soon realized that he faced an
enormous struggle.

When Policies Shut Out Example

Reynolds firmly believed that by setting the right example he could
change the way his eighty-five people did their jobs. His own example, he felt, could best motivate, stimulate, and guide his people
to more responsible activity than could any set of enforceable policies. No policy could make government less inefficient, ineffective,
and bureaucratic. In the beginning, Reynolds carefully mapped out
the values, beliefs, and principles that he thought could revolutionize the way people did things in his division. Then he developed a
scheme for modeling each of the values in his interaction with his
people. Extremely open with his managers about what he was trying
to accomplish, he explicitly recited the values and beliefs he himself
hoped would serve as a model for others. In this way, he hoped his
managers would do likewise with the people under them.

Then an amazing thing happened. People literally started
screaming that Reynolds was violating established agency policies
and should stop doing so or get out. Every time Reynolds attempted
to model a behavior and value that somehow contradicted a policy,
an outcry erupted, wherein people hotly contested the benefits of
the example versus those of established policy. For example, one of
the identified values was "we do whatever it takes to get the job
done right." Reynolds exemplified his commitment to this value by
working through a holiday to get a project completed. A group of
four other managers and staff had worked with him through the

holiday. According to agency policy, if an employee works on a holiday, he or she is eligible for one additional vacation day within the next twenty working days. The following week, Reynolds let the group know that he wasn't going to take the available "comp time" and implicitly encouraged them to follow his example. Since this was a crunch period for the division, Reynolds felt that getting the job done right meant going above and beyond the call of duty without expecting special compensation. When the managers and staff felt the pressure to follow Reynolds' example, they resisted and pulled out the policy manual to justify their position. As these kinds of situations accumulated, the managers within the division argued that Reynolds' noble aims might work in the private sector, but not in the federal government, where policy ruled. Before long, Reynolds became so frustrated, he called on me for help.

I suggested that we begin with an afternoon session with his management team where we could air out the issue. After the discussion session, I would follow up with a series of interviews with each manager. While the ensuing discussion and interviews revealed a willingness on the part of managers to try leading by example and by modeling behavior that supported values and beliefs, they feared that doing so would run counter to the current bureaucracy within the agency. One of them said flatly, "There's no room for leaders in government, only managers." Although I began to suspect the truth of this declaration, I felt sufficiently encouraged by Reynolds' conviction and devotion to move forward.

Together he and I decided to take an experimental tack with which we could test various combinations of leading by example and managing by policy. Theoretically, at least, the proper balance between the two could be just the ticket for this sticky situation.

When Example Applies Policy

Over the next several weeks, we tried numerous blends of example and policy. We tried to relate existing policies to values and beliefs; we tried to consolidate policies; we tried to incorporate values within policies; we even tried exemplifying policies. In the end, we discovered something rather interesting: The best blend involved using example to apply policy. Most people working in the federal government accepted policies as inviolate and therefore assumed you could only manage by them. Taking advantage of this fact, we introduced a subtle twist whereby example could determine how someone would apply a specific policy in a particular situation. This twist could overcome one of the biggest problems in government — that a rigid policy often gets in the way of effectiveness and problem solving. The right examples and models of appropriate and acceptable behavior based on key values could influence people to apply policies differently in different situations. Leaders then would have a place in government—a very important place. While managers could go on formulating and following policy, they could benefit from a leader's example of flexible policy application.

Policy and Example Really Can Live Together

After employing this blend over several months, people in the division became more creative, innovative, and more flexible as problem solvers. It wasn't long before the division heads and managers of other divisions began seeking Reynolds' advice on how to improve the performance of their own divisions. The word spread so rapidly throughout the federal agency that Reynolds was able to develop a workshop designed to teach managers how to use leading by example to enhance and improve the application of policy in a bureaucracy. The course made a big impact both inside Reynolds' division and throughout the agency.

Unfortunately for the federal government, Reynolds gained so much visibility in such a short time that one of the private contractors working with the agency made him an offer he couldn't refuse. He left the federal government. With him went much of the spark behind the new fire within the division. The new division head, a stickler for policy, took the division back into its old patterns and habits, much to the dismay of many of the people within it.

The most important thing I learned from this experience was that you can link leadership and management in even the toughest arenas, combining their best attributes to create a higher level of effectiveness than either one could ever achieve alone. However, you don't obtain the right blend by simply adding one to the other. You need to do a lot of struggling and experimenting before you hit the right combination. In fact, we stumbled on the notion that leading by example could help people apply policy while we were busy testing out quite a few other possibilities.

19

Instruction plus Inspiration

Managers Instruct; Leaders Inspire

Because managers want to make sure their people know how to do their jobs, they tend to issue *instructions*. To their minds, instruction and training represent some of their chief responsibilities. When they seek to increase productivity or commitment, they usually look first for opportunities to instruct and train their people. They emphasize the "hows" of individual and organizational performance. This does not mean that managers never attempt to inspire or explain the "whys"; they just don't think about them as much.

On the other hand, leaders, wanting to make sure their people know *why* their jobs are important, try harder to *inspire*. Inspiration and motivation, they believe, best help people grasp the meaning of their jobs. Once people understand this, they naturally become more productive and committed. Again, leaders certainly instruct their people in the "hows," but only after focusing on the "whys" and the attendant inspiration.

These two orientations played themselves out in a struggle between two executives who were acting as cochairmen for a major community development fund-raising campaign. One of the executives, the "trainer," was the managing partner of a big-eight CPA firm's local office, while the other, the "motivator," was CEO of a major construction company. The "trainer" displayed all the traits of a thoroughbred manager, among them an abiding belief in the power of instruction and training. The "motivator" possessed more of the characteristics of a leader, strongly feeling that inspiration could get people to put forth their best efforts. When the fund-raising campaign bogged down, both cochairmen became more actively involved in it, and that's when the sparks began to fly.

The Motivation Agenda

The city of approximately 800,000 people had never attempted such a large fund-raising campaign. It would use funds, garnished from corporate and individual contributors by a volunteer force of over 1000 workers, to build a huge cultural and entertainment arts complex near the downtown area. After six months of effort, however, the campaign had stalled. The army of volunteers had failed to reach any major target goals. When word began to leak that the campaign could be faltering, the reputations of the cochairmen went on the line. Both knew they needed to act quickly to stem the tide of public opinion and get citizens reaching for their wallets.

At a hastily scheduled meeting of the campaign's twelve-person steering committee, the cochairmen led a discussion on how to get the campaign back on track. As a member of the committee, I watched with interest as the cochairmen each promoted very different problem definitions and solutions. The "motivator" insisted that the 1000 plus volunteers simply lacked sufficient motivation and desperately needed to be fired up. He waxed eloquent in his description of how to get each volunteer to embrace the shining vision of the new cultural and entertainment arts complex which he or she could then pass on to the community at large: "Excitement and enthusiasm, that's what we need!" To set the fire burning, he proposed a series of volunteer rallies to keep fervor at a high pitch during the next six months. He also recommended that we bring in motivational speakers to rally the troops.

The Training Agenda

Next, the "trainer" took the floor. As much as I dislike stereotyping businesspeople, this person did personify the detail-oriented, procedure-driven "bean counter" many people imagine when they think of accountants. While he agreed with his cochairman about the need to motivate and inspire workers, it became more and more obvious as the meeting wore on that he made this acknowledgment only out of polite deference. In reality, he believed that the volunteers simply lacked the necessary know-how to raise money. To combat this problem, he suggested that we hire professional fund raisers to instruct the volunteers: "And we need a very clear fund-raising procedure everyone can follow."

When Equal Balance Won't Work

As the meeting wound down, I noted that we had spent a great deal of time doing little more than debate the relative merits of instruction versus inspiration. Some of us on the steering committee, feeling less adamant about one or the other, had shifted back and forth between them. In an act of desperation, someone finally proposed a balanced approach, including both instruction and inspiration. When even this compromise evoked misgivings, one fellow steering committee member asked for my opinion.

I started out by saying, "I think we've thoroughly discussed all the major issues facing this fund-raising campaign. Now, what we need, more than anything else, is a clear, unwavering commitment to one approach or the other." If it were strictly up to me, I told them, I would take the inspiration route. I saw no need for more instruction than a one-page summary of fund-raising guidelines. What the volunteers needed more than anything was to feel inspired to do whatever it took to raise the required monies. Once the vision of what the cultural and entertainment arts complex would do for the community, their children, and the social atmosphere came alive for each volunteer, that vision could spread like wildfire throughout the community.

Finally, we took a vote, with ten of twelve voting for an inspirational course of action. Immediately we formed a subcommittee to develop a plan and schedule its presentation to the full steering committee for approval and implementation the following week.

My own busy schedule took me away from the campaign for a few months. Then one day a fellow member of the steering committee called to say the campaign had not only reached but exceeded its goals. "The inspiration strategy worked like a charm," he said. "The effort seems to have revitalized the entire community." He also noted, with a chuckle, that the "trainer" had subtly tried to distance himself from the campaign, letting the "motivator" take the lead, until the campaign started looking like a real success. Then, he got heavily involved in the effort himself. My friend concluded, "I think even our bean counter friend got inspired!"

In another situation, you may need to emphasize instruction. For example, in the area of fund raising, you may already have sufficient inspiration and motivation on the part of both fund raiser and donor but need to utilize some sophisticated techniques or vehicles such as trust funds, grants, or "in-kind" donations to make the campaign work. This would require more emphasis on instruction. Either way, one will probably be emphasized over the other, even though both are always necessary.

20

MBO
plus
MBWA

Managers MBO; Leaders MBWA

MBO, a term coined by George Odiorne several years ago, stands for "management by objectives." *MBWA*, a term popularized by Tom Peters and Bob Waterman, stands for "management by walking around." Managers, who like to set goals and measure progress toward them, love MBO because this approach ensures tangible, graspable, clearly identifiable objectives. Because MBO allows managers to make people in the organization accountable for accomplishing specific objectives, this approach comforts managers, who want to see that people and the organization are moving along the right track.

On the other hand, leaders, who like to get a feel for the way people perform in daily situations, derive a lot more comfort from MBWA. Leaders like to assess first hand what's really happening in their organizations, and they can accomplish this best by literally walking around, talking to people, and remaining in constant contact with the flesh and blood of the organization. Unlike managers, who prefer to develop hierarchies of objectives, all relating back to a set of overall objectives, leaders would rather establish a common purpose or philosophy and then stay in touch with people throughout the organization to make sure that they work in sync with that guiding purpose.

In reality, the best organizations employ people who are both MBO and MBWA, because both approaches can help achieve an organization's overriding purpose and collective objectives. Those comfortable with one approach can and should grow more comfortable with the other. Let's see how.

MBO Only

Some time ago one of my business partners and I became involved with a 100-year-old, midsized manufacturer of industrial products that was striving to update and modernize its approach to management. Although the company enjoyed a long history of competitive advantage in the marketplace, it had recently suffered through a trying two-year period during which it had laid off many employees and had undertaken a lot of streamlining and down-sizing. When we became involved with the organization, it had just begun to emerge from this difficult period and was starting to look for new, fresh ways to increase managerial effectiveness. The CEO, our client and main contact during the course of our consulting, was the company's former chief financial officer and was heavily biased toward finance, accounting, and the quantitative side of business. He took great delight in clearly laying out the company's objectives and goals, convincing each of his subordinates of their importance, and then watching everyone move forward to accomplish them. To cement this commitment to MBO throughout his organization, he insisted that his subordinates manage their subordinates the same way.

From the point of view of goals and objectives, this organization appeared to be extremely well directed. Everyone seemed to be marching to the beat of the MBO drum. However, during some of our interviews with key people, it became clear that many felt hampered by a lack of communication and interaction with management regarding how to specifically go about achieving certain goals and objectives. For his part, the CEO, who assumed that once his managers accepted a set of objectives, their people should be able to accomplish them, expressed frustration over the fact that many of his managers lacked the high levels of initiative and accountability he expected. He could not understand why his managers weren't making things happen and realizing their objectives. Expectations were abundantly clear, yet performance was sometimes disappointing.

MBWA Only

To this we responded that he could expect little more in light of his own lack of interaction with his managers once goals and objectives were set. Ongoing communication, including frequent face-to-face discussion of precisely how to accomplish goals, how to remove obstacles, and how to solve problems and make decisions associated with the goals, simply did not occur in this organization. After many interviews, the CEO ultimately agreed that he needed to loosen the reins on management through objectives. To help him understand why MBO only or MBWA only caused problems, we cited the story of another executive who had focused only on MBWA. As the MBWA-only company grew, it became more and more difficult for this leader to maintain contact with everyone in the organization, until he found that the company ran very well only when he was in town and close to his people. This happened because his presence served to clarify expectations and to inspire, initiate, and provide feedback. He provided the glue that held things together. However, when he was out of town, which occurred more and more frequently as the company grew, the organization seemed to come to a standstill. In his absence, people, who depended so much on his MBWA, lost their framework for proceeding on their own. Interestingly, this leader, like our CEO client, found that his people also lacked the initiative and accountability he desired. In the end, MBWA alone can cause the same kind of low-level initiative and lack of accountability that MBO alone creates.

MBO plus MBWA

In the MBO-only situation, the CEO had remained too aloof from the management process. However, once he realized the need for more direct involvement with managers who reported to him, he turned the situation around rather quickly. Luckily, this organization had developed a very strong internal technical competence and an admirable ability to deliver the products needed by customers. What it lacked was managerial competence. When it had grown larger, this fact posed more and more of an obstacle to the firm's continued progress.

The CEO and his management team started to augment MBO with MBWA. Their efforts included more frequent meetings, regular visits to plant locations and branch offices, and informal get-togethers. They also spent more time getting out of the executive suite, mingling with employees and talking to them about what they were doing and what problems they faced when working toward the organization's objectives. At the same time, they tried to develop participative management skills, allowing for a good deal of give and take with people. They worked hard to communicate and reinforce a high level of trust and mutual benefit.

Results came quickly, but not that easily. In the beginning, the CEO wasn't consistent with MBWA, apparently because he did not feel comfortable with such a markedly different style. However, he enlisted the help of those leaders among the management team who were more oriented toward MBWA. They became the informal stewards of MBWA and began to receive immediate and strong positive feedback. Not only did people appreciate their efforts, they also began to understand and relate to the company's objectives even more. At first, the employees had responded to the CEO's efforts as they would to a PR campaign, but as the process continued, their interchanges with the CEO and other executives became more and more meaningful. The program helped everyone blend the common purpose of the organization with individual and group objectives. As a result, a new sense of energy and commitment swept into the organization over a period of months.

In the case of MBO and MBWA, it doesn't matter whether

you're a manager or a leader. You need to make sure your organization benefits from both. If a CEO or organization head never projects an overriding mission or purpose that can guide the organization, then he or she will inevitably lose influence with people as the organization grows larger. Eventually, it becomes virtually impossible to influence everyone in the organization personally. To counteract this effect, you can help your managers become more oriented toward MBWA and thus extend your influence through the organization. Of course, you will have to give your managers some guidelines and examples of how they can employ MBWA most effectively; otherwise they may just go through the motions. At the same time, the CEO or organization head must use MBO to develop clear objectives, which enable people to get things done on a functional level. Objectives must, of course, relate to the overall purpose of the organization and be developed at all levels of the organization. When this happens, MBO can greatly enhance the power of MBWA.

21

Control plus Empower

Managers Control; Leaders Empower

Managers generally think in terms of *controlling* the elements of an organization's culture, strategy and all the other variables that fall within their domain. To control, they assume, is to maximize. When it comes to people, the manager assumes that people also need to be controlled. Control, managers feel, will help people attain the co-operation the organization requires. In the manager's mind, if you can't control it, you can't manage it.

Leaders, in sharp contrast, would rather *empower* organizations and people. To their way of thinking, empowerment can unleash the energy necessary to take the organization beyond its current position. Only by giving people the freedom and resources to act can you expect them to go above and beyond the call of duty. Leaders empower people, systems, structures, strategies, and other variables by opening the way for their expansion, enhancement, and evolution. The leader's soul says, "If you can't empower, you can't lead."

A good example of this cropped up when I worked with one of the offices of a large international consulting firm, where two principals oversaw different areas of the consulting practice, each with its own staff. These two principals couldn't have run their operations more differently.

The Controlling Principal

One principal, I'll call him Jack, carefully watched, supervised, and directed all activities of his staff who provided financial analysis and systems implementation services to its clients. When anyone wrote up a proposal, Jack carefully controlled every step in the process, including mandatory daily and sometimes hourly updates. When someone went out to work for a client, Jack insisted that the job be meticulously planned beforehand and then carried out accordingly, with little deviation. Working papers documenting each step of the project also were carefully prepared and reviewed to ensure that nothing went wrong. Realizing the importance of relationships with clients, Jack got personally involved with every single client in his practice area. As a result of all this control, his group's services enjoyed a reputation for being precise and well supervised.

Clients and potential clients within the group's market area highly respected its capabilities. In fact, Jack's team won almost all the business it went after. The precision with which it operated produced consulting advice clients could easily implement and control within their own organizations. Someone observing Jack's success might even call his approach a model for consulting success.

The Empowering Principal

The other principal, I'll refer to her as Jane, went about building her consulting practice in quite the opposite way. A leader by instinct, Jane always tried to empower her people to develop their own creative capabilities and follow their own courses. Since her consulting practice covered a broad area, her staff enjoyed a range of opportunities from marketing strategy to organizational design. Reporting to her were four practice area leaders, with their own staffs, who operated autonomously from one another. Since Jane encouraged her subordinates to operate the way she did, no two groups functioned the same way. Each developed different approaches to the market, distinct methods of relating to their clients, and unique ways of delivering their services. The principal herself did not get involved in details. Rather, she monitored the growth and profitability of each of the practice areas, constantly encouraging each of her lead consultants to do whatever he or she thought best to meet client needs and seize market opportunities. The practice had built a strong reputation for creativity, and clients often boasted that they got from the group the sorts of unusual and tailor-made recommendations that could quickly sprint them out ahead of their competitors. As with Jack's team, someone observing Jane's group could hold it up as a model for consulting success.

To Control or to Empower, That Is the Question

Needless to say, these two principals often tangled in office management meetings. While Jane would never dream of placing "straitjackets" on her people, Jack could not understand how Jane could let her practice "run wild." Obviously, each could claim success with his or her approach, but neither could appreciate the other's skills.

When I evaluated the two practices for the office-managing partner, I concluded that he should do little to change either principal's attitude or behavior, provided their areas of responsibility did not change.

Jack, it turned out, held responsibility for areas dependent on technical competence and expertise, ones that lent themselves to a controlling approach. On the other hand, Jane directed practice areas that depended more on business development and responsiveness to market opportunities, trends, and developments, areas

that required flexibility and creativity. Jack would surely kill practice areas that required these traits. At the same time, Jane would
have run into monumental problems with a freewheeling approach
in areas that demanded precision and technical expertise. Both
these principals' areas of responsibility were critical to the overall
well-being of the office, and the office-managing partner wisely
valued their contrasting orientations and contributing roles in the
overall scheme of things.

I had been asked to help the international headquarters office
identify exactly what was happening within this record-setting
branch office so that it could become a model for the whole firm. My
final report urged the firm to tailor the controlling and empowering
orientations within given offices to the areas where they would
create the most value. Specifically, I recommended that practice
areas dealing with financial analysis, cost accounting, systems design and implementation, performance reviews, and management
audits be led by principals more oriented toward control. Those
practice areas dealing with marketing or business strategy, corporate culture, innovation and product development, management
training and development, and leadership improvement should be
led by principles more oriented toward empowerment. Finally,
those dealing with marketing analysis, business planning, organizational analysis and design, compensation studies, and human
resource consulting should be led by principals more balanced or
less extreme in their orientation toward control or empowerment.
In short, CEOs, managing partners, and anyone else who has overall responsibility for an organization should carefully identify
where, when, and how to employ the controlling and empowering
orientations and then make sure that appropriate managers and
leaders deliver the orientation required by particular activities.

22

Releasing plus Keeping

Managers Easily Release People; Leaders Would Rather Keep Them

Obviously, managers and leaders can both fire and hold onto people. However, when things aren't going right in an organization in terms of the strength of the culture or the organization's capabilities, managers can fairly easily *release* people and start with a fresh, new set. Inherently, managers seem to credit people with a limited ability to change and develop. Once people reach that limit, despite circumstances that require more changes, you frequently have to terminate them. For this reason, managers, on their own, usually find it difficult to renew corporate cultures, unless they can do so with firings and layoffs.

Leaders facing the same circumstances would rather *keep* the people, working with, training, and further developing them. In this regard, leaders display more skill at creating corporate cultures than do managers because creating a corporate culture often requires people to be flexible and adaptive. Leaders believe people can change dramatically. However, sometimes leaders fail to renew corporate cultures because they hold on too long to people who are unwilling to change.

The president and CEO of a medium-sized manufacturing and service company had surrounded himself with a cadre of very outspoken vice presidents and managers. Four of these managers reported to a vice president for whom they held little respect. The relationships in the situation had deteriorated so much that three of the four managers were going around the vice president and directly to the president to resolve issues and make decisions. The managers had become so frustrated over time that they began implying that the vice president should be asked to resign.

The president, on the other hand, respected the vice president and resisted terminating him without giving him adequate opportunity to resolve the conflict with his people. After the president conducted several one-on-one sessions with the vice president, he himself saw less progress than he had hoped for. However, the president wanted to give the vice president an adequate chance to change not only because of the latter's past contribution to the company, but also because he held a portion of stock in the company. The four dissidents who reported to the vice president also were valuable members of the management group and potential future officers of the company. Two of them also owned stock.

At this point, the president asked me to design a series of retreats that would focus the executive group's (senior officers and the next level of management) attention on the company's values, culture, and strategic direction. Among other goals, he wanted to get the tension between the vice president and his lieutenants out into the open. Since this situation conflicted with what the organization stood for, the president wanted to use these retreats as an opportunity to bring fresh air into relationships and provide an example to other members of the executive group.

Release Him

Prior to the first retreat, I interviewed each participant to assess his or her view of the current situation and gain background and an understanding that would help me structure all the retreat sessions. During interviews with the four circumventing managers, I heard a resounding cry for the termination or reassignment of the vice president. Probing more deeply into this feedback, I discovered that the managers really held the vice president in contempt. No one thought he could possibly change, at least not quickly or completely enough. I repeatedly asked one question during these interviews, "If he could change, then could you respect him?" Every time the answer came, "He can't, so I can't." When I pressed one of them harder, he answered, "Well, *maybe*." However, I was not surprised to hear each of these managers express an impulse to fire or terminate anyone who could not change to the managers' satisfaction.

Keep Him

After the interviews, I met with the president to discuss the agenda for the retreat. In the process, I shared what I'd picked up from my interviews. Without divulging who had said what, I sketched the almost unanimous feeling that the vice president should go. The president indicated that he could not with good conscience terminate the vice president yet. He still felt the vice president could change but somehow had just not received the right motivation or guidance to do so. "I want to keep him," concluded the president. "I just need to find the right way to help him resolve the conflict in his group." When the president then asked me whether I agreed with his decision to work with the vice president, I told him I didn't think he could live with himself if he did anything less.

Go the Extra Mile

The retreat began, and after two grueling days during which we dragged a lot of sensitive issues, concerns, and feelings out on the table, some people began to confide in me their fear that we had opened up some wounds that would never heal. The managers' bitter criticisms of the vice president had been particularly painful, and it was clear to me that both the vice president and the attacking managers needed to make some changes. After the first two-day session, the president spoke with all who had attended in an effort to determine how productive they had found the experience. To his relief, he discovered a new commitment to change by both the vice president and his outspokenly critical managers. Said one, "We've needed this openness for a long time, even though it hurt to get it started." Prior to the retreat, apparently, no one felt comfortable confronting anyone else with such a problem, which permitted a lot of hidden agendas and office politics to arise.

The vice president and his group agreed to hold a series of sessions, at first with the president, and then on their own, to make the individual and group changes they felt necessary at this point. During those subsequent meetings, communication and camaraderie seemed to improve. The vice president did change, albeit slowly, and so did the managers who reported to him. It didn't happen magically at the retreat, although that occasion did initiate the process. Never before had the vice president been confronted so directly with the concerns of those reporting to him. Also, never had the managers felt free to express their dissatisfaction so clearly. Slowly, but surely, the respect between the vice president and his lieutenants seemed to get better. Unfortunately, many months later, the vice president's willingness to change came to a halt. Resenting the pressure to change, he fell back into old habits and began defensively justifying his behavior and decisions. He was fired.

Change isn't easy for anyone, but organizations that afford people the opportunity to change will find that they tap even deeper levels of commitment and fulfillment. When building an organizational culture, you will surely need to fire some people along the way, but you'll be wise to go the second mile to help an individual change. One changed individual, as a result of patient, sensitive leadership, will change ten more as his or her story of change becomes a beacon of trust and commitment throughout the organization. However, one individual unwilling to change will cause ten others to assume a similar posture, weakening commitment and trust throughout the organization. Only a blend of management and leadership can strike the right balance between releasing and keeping.

23

Consistency plus Commitment

Managers Employ Consistency; Leaders Elicit Commitment

Culture building, to a manager, translates into *consistency*. Consistency breeds predictability and hence trust among employees. It provides the steady drum beat to which any great corporation marches year after year. The leader, less keen on predictability, sees *commitment* as the real music to which the corporate culture dances. Commitment provides the central theme that builds trust among employees.

A Fortune 500 food-processing company that prides itself on human resource management through the help of numerous Ph.D.s presumably on the leading edge of thought and practice in the area, invited me to conduct a one-day workshop. During the workshop, I discovered an interesting debate among these human resource professionals over the relative importance of consistent practices and high levels of commitment among an organization's people.

Be Consistent

Those who put forth the consistency argument, led by a savvy veteran I'll call Steinberg, insisted that practices congruent with the company's values naturally forge high levels of commitment among employees. According to Steinberg, people would flounder if they could not predict and count on consistent practices. Although he agreed on the importance of commitment in any vibrant and strong corporate culture, he saw the path to commitment paved with consistency. To support his contention, he brought out studies from inside the company that proved how years of consistent practices, priorities, and approaches had instilled great commitment. In particular, he cited the company's performance evaluation system as a consistent practice that over the years had developed better and better managers throughout the organization. Because the company had been so consistent and even dogmatic in its implementation of this performance evaluation system, a commitment to performance evaluation had grown steadily over the years.

Be Committed

The other side of the debate argued that commitment came first. Their informal leader was an articulate advocate I'll call Whiteside. While Whiteside conceded that consistency does, in fact, play a key role in any strong organization, the idea that consistency precedes commitment grossly distorts reality and sidetracks the drive toward high levels of commitment among employees. To his mind, consistency came about as a byproduct of commitment, not vice versa. A strong corporate culture, Whiteside insisted, invariably springs from commitment to a central idea, common purpose, or transcendent vision that can remain constant, even in the face of wrenching change. He also used the same example of performance evaluation, arguing that the performance evaluation system only existed because of a deep commitment within the company to people development. No consistent practice, no well-developed performance evaluation system would have arisen had it not been preceded by a deep and abiding commitment to the notion of high-quality people development.

The Bond Between Consistency and Commitment

During the workshop, I spent a great deal of time teasing out the main points of this debate because it seemed to me to sit at the heart of the workshop's topic: how to identify and manage the elements of a strong, successful, vibrant organizational culture. After I had helped clarify the debate, I urged the two sides to find some way to resolve their apparent disagreement. Unless they did, I felt the company would not be able to build an even stronger culture because it would be sending mixed signals to employees. When, after several hours of discussion, each side seemed even more entrenched in its particular point of view, I dusted off the old "chicken and egg" analogy: "Instead of fighting over which comes first, why not agree that you can't have one without the other?" This question was an obvious one, but nevertheless, it seemed to strike a chord, and after more discussion, both sides agreed that it made sense never to discuss commitment without talking about consistency, and vice versa. Steinberg summarized it best when he suggested that while the debate had helped crystalize the two positions, the discussion should now turn to integrating the two positions. As the group became more resolution-oriented and less argumentative, they began discussing how to create a natural bond between the "chicken" of consistency and the "egg" of commitment. In the end, they formulated an approach to culture building that instead of pitting the two elements against one another, bound them together as equals. Employees within the company needed both.

The preliminary plan for strengthening the company's culture went something like this: If you focus only on consistency as the driving force behind a strong culture and its commitment, you risk becoming too attached to consistent practices that may prevent you from adapting to dynamic changes in the environment and thus may weaken, not strengthen, your culture. On the other hand, if you focus only on commitment as the key to a strong culture, with consistent practices as a mere byproduct, that commitment can become too intangible and hard to grasp. Therefore, we must deal with both, equally and simultaneously. In other words, commitment manifests itself in consistent practices but is not constrained by them. Likewise, consistent practices sustain commitment but do not stifle it. In this particular company's case, commitment to producing quality products manifests itself in consistent practices such as total quality procedures, quality circles, quality assurance training and zero-rejects programs. But none of these practices fully captures the attitude toward a total quality work environment felt by committed employees. This attitude will create the consistent practices of the future. And that's how one plus one equals three.

IV

External/ Internal Change

The future promises enormous accelerating change, and only those organizations which effectively handle such change, both externally and internally, will prosper in the decade ahead. This variable alone will weed out the weak from the strong. As with other success factors, managers and leaders deal with change quite differently. Managers, especially in management-dominated organizations, strive continually to achieve stability in their organizations. In the world of constant and rapid change, however, stability can quickly turn into stagnation. Leaders, on the other hand, love to introduce change into their organizations, constantly creating new directions, agendas, and priorities that, particularly in leadership-driven organizations, can create a state of continual crisis.

The conflict-oriented organization attempts to balance stability and crisis by pitting managers against leaders, while the vacillation-prone organization deliberately shifts between the two. Only in balanced and integrated organizations do managers and leaders combine in such a way as to permit stability and crisis to flow into one another, smoothly and productively.

In this section you will see how managers and leaders approach change differently. As you read the various cases, try to keep in mind the need to blend the two orientations together in a balanced and integrated way. Remember, in the best organizations, managers and leaders work side by side, combining constant change with changelessness to produce the best environment for success.

24

Stability plus Crisis

Managers Yearn for Stability; Leaders Thrive on Crisis

Security-minded managers naturally prefer *stability* over crisis, because to a manager's mind, the "stable state" with its accompanying order, discipline, regimen, and predictable performance represents the ideal. Stability doesn't necessarily imply stagnation or the inability to change, however. Rather, it means calm and reasoned progress through change. During times of crisis, the manager thinks hardest about somehow reestablishing stability.

Leaders prefer *crisis* over stability. In the turmoil that surrounds a crisis, the leader feels heartened that things are happening. For the leader's soul, crisis doesn't mean chaos, but rather a breakthrough close at hand. During times of stability, a leader often grows bored, restless for the next crisis that will propel the organization to new heights. If no crisis erupts, the leader will most likely create one.

I recently took part in a two-day conference with a well-known food company whose products abound today in most homes in America and throughout the world. Having grown rapidly over the last twenty years, the company, a major division of a larger parent organization, currently racks up sales of about $1 billion a year. During the two-day conference, the subject of change and its impact on strategy and culture came up again and again. In one session in particular, we began to probe into the issue in some detail. In the course of a rather intense discussion, we dissected the fact that two product areas within the company operate very differently in the marketplace, and yet utilize the same marketing, sales, and general staff support. One product group enjoyed a large market share in a mature and stable market, while the other was competing in a fast-growth market with a smaller, but growing share. The one product was characterized by stability; the other, by crisis. As we continued our discussion, it became apparent that the company desperately needed a way of thinking about change that would help it solve problems in widely different circumstances.

Going for Stability When You Should Be Going for Crisis

The stable product group, producing canned products with a solid reputation and high customer loyalty, had enjoyed a long history of steady growth. The volatile product group was undergoing rapid development and was beset by crisis after crisis. While both product groups used similar ingredients, the latter had targeted the pet food market. The problem? All the executives of the company wanted nothing more than to establish stability for both product groupings, even the one operating in a sea of crisis. The combined marketing, financial planning, sales, and other staff support functions, guided by those at the top, all drove toward programs, policies, procedures, and systems that would supposedly bring stability. As I guided the discussion toward the differences between managers and leaders and their handling of stability and crisis, the group began to see that the crisis surrounding the one product area was not inherently bad, but rather characteristic of the marketplace it served. However, their habitual "stability" response was bad because it could not work for the volatile product group.

By the end of the first day, the executive group agreed that it needed to approach the volatile product area more appropriately and effectively. Since the person primarily responsible for it was a natural leader, he lit up like a Christmas tree at this suggestion. Not only could he foresee an end to his frustration within the company, he now possessed a framework for thinking about the problems he was experiencing with his group. What a relief to stop formulating policies, systems, procedures, and programs designed to bring about stability and start working instead on the innovation, adaptability, flexibility, and quickness that would turn the crisis into a positive situation.

Going with Crisis When You Should Be Going with Stability

When the conference reconvened the next morning, we reviewed the previous afternoon's discussions to see if we still supported the conclusions we had drawn. With insight and clarity, the leader of the product area in crisis asked if he could diagram some of his thoughts. Using the stability and crisis framework that we had talked about the previous day, he charted where every product line in the company stood — either in the midst of stability, pursuing stability, or in the midst of crisis. Of course, he identified the two product groups that represented the company's major sources of revenue and profitability, but he also included other minor product lines. He then diagramed how businesses tend to move in and out of stability and crisis modes. Using the history of the more stable product area to illustrate a business that had endured both stability and crisis, he suggested that a time might come in the future when the stable product area could itself experience crisis conditions again. A time also would probably come when his own product area would enter an era of stability, probably four to seven years down the road. At that time, each product area would need a very different approach than it required now.

After the first speaker sat down, another manager offered an insight. He said that he had witnessed occasions when a crisis-oriented leader had been put in charge of a stable business and had actually hurt the market position of that business by introducing

radical changes in strategic direction or operating policies that became counterproductive to the company's long-term viability. I
agreed. "What any multiproduct company needs is a careful ongoing assessment of each product line or product group to determine
its position on the stability/crisis continuum. The positions will tell
you when to manage and when to lead."

The conference ended with this company's management
group feeling that it had reached some important conclusions about
the business.

Let the Situation Be Your Guide

All organizations experience times of both stability and crisis in their
histories. In fact, the times of stability often mark resting points or
strengthening periods before crisis comes around again. By the
same token, periods of crisis often represent opportunities for major
leaps forward. An organization in the midst of a period of stability
does not need a leader inflicting crisis on it, nor does an organization in the midst of crisis need a manager enforcing stability on it.
However, a long period of stability can signal stagnation, at which
point the injection of a leader and a dose of crisis can be a very
healthy thing. For an organization that has battled so much crisis
that it tends to create additional crises for no good reason, a manager and a treatment of calm, steady strengthening can be just what
the doctor ordered.

25

Duplicate plus Originate

Managers Duplicate; Leaders Originate

Managers generally prefer the most efficient and effective paths toward goals, an orientation that often entails *duplicating*, copying, or using someone else's idea, system, or design. "Why," asks the manager, "should I reinvent the wheel?" The manager would, in a sense, opt for a reliable, proven car rather than a new-fangled vehicle not yet tested on the road. To a person with this mind set, duplicating another organization's approach makes much more sense than originating something new, because borrowing is faster, easier, more effective, and cheaper than starting from scratch.

The leader, however, yearns for the opportunity to *originate* or invent something new. Convinced that breakthrough thinking creates the sharpest competitive edge, the leader continually searches for brand new ways of doing something. "Why rely on wheels," asks the leader, "when you can invent a better mode of travel?" Whether developing a new product, restructuring an organization, redesigning an incentive compensation system, or forging global alliances, the leader believes that the long-term advantage lies in originality.

For a number of years now I have directly and indirectly studied the growth and development of a premier high-tech company on the leading edge of its field: computer simulation of real-life situations and occurrences. For years, SimuTech (not its real name) has struggled for a balance between duplicating and originating, and the dilemma continues to plague it almost every day, with battle lines clearly drawn. The duplicators work mostly in the marketing and manufacturing side of the business. The originators reside more on the R&D and engineering side.

The Duplicators

The managers at SimuTech, usually those in marketing and manufacturing, argue that the company sacrificed millions of dollars in revenue and profit when it refused to mass produce its technological innovations. To support this contention, they point to competitors who have always waited in the wings, observing SimuTech's breakthroughs and then duplicating and mass producing them. These rivals, they argue, have grown a lot faster and have made a lot more money because they have exploited existing technology or technology developed by someone else. "We've led the field in originality long enough," insisted one vice president, "but that doesn't pay the bills around here. Let's get off our high horses and get down into the trenches where the other guys are getting rich." Most of SimuTech's other managers agree that although the company enjoys great respect in the industry as a state-of-the-art leader, that respect hasn't brought big market share, growth, and profits.

These managers would rather see the company back off its preoccupation with originality and focus on just two or three high-growth, high-profit product/market areas where it could become the dominant competitor quite quickly. Then the company could defend its dominant market positions by quickly duplicating or copying future technological developments as they come along. This strategy, argue the managers, would make much more business sense and, in the long run, could even better fund the sort of basic R&D the company currently cherishes. In the short to medium term (two to seven years), the company could surely lose its leading-edge position, but it might well get it back once it refocused on R&D down the road. "Even if it doesn't," claimed the outspoken vice president, "it would at least be a major force in the industry rather than simply a respected contributor."

The Originators

The leaders in this company, mostly engineers and scientists, strongly disagree. "Why," they ask, "should a company that has won recognition as the technological leader in its field want to toss that position aside for the sake of more growth and profits?" Although any firm can duplicate another's innovations, they say, only a few can consistently innovate themselves. Should SimuTech grow more rapidly or reap more profits just to keep the marketers happy? After all, the company's bottom line is respectable, and a bigger firm is not necessarily a better firm.

The leaders make a strong case for continuing to focus on the development of prototypes and customized product applications for major government and private industry use rather than getting into the business of mass marketing specific products. If the company decided to mass produce for a few years, they argue, creating a lot of profit that might even fund more future R&D, the company would lose its leading-edge position and probably never regain it. Key creative people would leave, the entire corporate culture would change, and the hard-won position of consistent technological innovation would evaporate. No amount of money could re-create the company's present position. "If we lose that," says one top scientist, "we lose the very essence of who we are."

"Divided We Stand"

Sometimes it's not possible to blend warring management and leadership viewpoints, and continued efforts to do so may produce even more disruptive conflict. In the case of SimuTech, the marketers' arguments did help the engineers and scientists pay closer attention to the needs of customers when developing product prototypes and customized product applications. And the engineers' and scientists' position did strengthen the marketers' appreciation of the power of reputation and respect gained by constantly staying on the leading technological edge. However, the marketers would forever want to cash in on the reputation by moving into a duplicating mode, hoping to fund R&D in the future. For their part, the engineers and scientists would forever resist the mass marketing, duplication alternative as a materialistic, greedy compromise of principles and genuine progress.

After spending a good deal of time listening to both sides, I finally offered them a solution they had not expected. Each side assumed one or the other would win, but that would, obviously, make one side the loser. Emphasizing, instead, a win-win approach, I suggested that SimuTech *not* completely relieve the tension between marketing and engineering. Such tension is positive, provided it does not lead to disruptive squabbling, ultimatums, and resignations. Many companies, I pointed out, cycle through phases of low tension and high tension. To keep the tension positive, I recommended that SimuTech create two sister companies, one to focus on mass-market products and applications and the other to focus on state-of-the-art technological development. This would allow some blending of the manager and leader perspectives, but it also would better recognize the fundamental differences between the two. The marketers who leaned toward the engineering side would go with the technological development-focused company, while the engineers and scientists who leaned toward the marketing side would go with the mass marketing–focused company. In order to maintain positive tension and a productive blending of the two orientations, I urged the new units to develop systems for communicating and coordinating between themselves.

Sometimes separation takes advantage of the strengths of both managers and leaders. Both duplicating and originating perspectives can benefit most companies. But since the two can seldom hammer out a mutually agreeable compromise under one roof, it often makes sense for them to operate under two separate roofs. In general, I suggest that the originating and duplicating orientations should be separated in any organization, whether through subsidiaries or individual companies, when two conditions exist: (1) the organization can successfully pursue both originating and duplicating strategies in the marketplace, and (2) the strategic positions of originating and duplicating substantially differ from each other.

When these two conditions are not present, the organization will most likely have to choose an orientation, duplicating or originating, to primarily guide its strategic direction. Both orientations, equally emphasized, will only generate conflict.

26

Fasten
plus
Unfasten

Managers Fasten Things Down; Leaders Unfasten Them

Managers *fasten* in two ways. First, they fasten their attention on specific issues, and then they try to fasten resolutions to those issues down on the organization. When they look at a forest, they see individual trees. As a result, managers constantly set priorities, objectives, milestones, assignments, expectations, and any other specific and concrete factors that lead toward goals. Such phrases as "get a fix on," "lock in on," "tie down," and "nail down" pervade the language of managers. When they cannot easily "lock in on" an issue or "nail down" a resolution, they grow uncomfortable.

By the same token, leaders *unfasten* in two ways. First, they like to unfocus their gaze, letting immediate concerns blur so that they can grasp the larger context, and then they try to unfasten tied-down aspects of their organizations. When they see a tree, they imagine a forest. In this way, leaders often disdain existing directions, priorities, objectives, tasks and expectations. Leaders question the potentially myopic, narrow views of the marketplace, customers, competitors, and past organizational responses in an effort to avoid ruts, bad habits or other unproductive traditions. The vocabulary of leaders includes such phrases as "loosen up," "stand back and take stock," "look at the big picture," and "shake things up." When leaders cannot "loosen things up," they become anxious.

OmniCare (a fictitious name) owns and operates specialty health care facilities such as psychiatric hospitals, extended care units, and rest homes. The chairman and CEO of the company, George Karas (not his real name), is a strong leader who regularly "shakes things up" by changing organizational priorities, meeting agendas, or anything else that seems too securely locked in place. The president and COO of the company, Raymond Martin (not his real name), is a strong manager who likes to lock things securely in place. Not surprisingly, conflict at the top of the organization has sparked many heated debates, some of which have turned out well and others of which have turned out badly. On one occasion, the senior executive team had been working on a new market thrust for several weeks under Raymond's direction with what he thought was George's blessing only to have the rug pulled out from underneath him when George said he felt the company would make a bad mistake if it plunged into that particular market.

When the Fastening/Unfastening Combination Works

At OmniCare, the fastening/unfastening combination seems to work beautifully when George Karas restricts unfastening to the external environment and Raymond Martin confines fastening to the organization's internal environment. Only then does each seem to appreciate the other's approach. For example, George enjoys a deserved reputation in his industry as a major innovator of patient services. Unafraid to pursue unconventional, nontraditional, and unprecedented courses of action, George has successfully created a number of new market segments and an unparalleled level of customer service. He also has negotiated innovative alliances, joint ventures, and mergers with other companies and facilities for the growth and benefit of Omni-Care stakeholders. In particular, he developed the concept of "continuum of care," referring to a continuum of health care services in the psychiatric area ranging from intensive care to occasional care, that has become a standard in the industry.

By the same token, Raymond has won equal distinction for developing and implementing the internal operating policies, management systems, and organizational processes that have turned George's visions into profitable realities. Over the years, Raymond has demonstrated a flair for modifying and adjusting internal operations and facilities to take advantage of the external environment changes, acquisitions, and joint ventures.

When George focuses outside and Raymond focuses inside, all goes well. Unfortunately, however, they cannot always maintain such clear-cut boundaries.

When the Fastening/Unfastening Combination Fails

As happens with almost any leader, George Karas cannot always restrict himself to the external environment, nor can Raymond Martin always confine his efforts to the internal situation. Whenever George does turn his attention to the internal workings of the company, unfastening things at will, the organization usually plunges into a state of confusion as it struggles to accommodate change while still implementing company policy. On one occasion, Raymond had been gradually implementing a carefully thought-out, new regional organizational structure in a particular part of the company when George paid a surprise visit to the region in question and unilaterally introduced a totally different organizational approach. As a result, the region wallowed in a chaotic mess for months until Raymond finally smoothed things out by implementing a hybrid of the two organizational approaches.

On the other side of the coin, George had at one time been deeply involved in discussions with a company he was interested in acquiring. When he asked Raymond to tackle the specifics of how they could best meld the acquired company into existing operations, Raymond did so gladly. But after a few weeks, Raymond became convinced that the whole undertaking made no strategic sense. His communication of this attitude to the management of the target acquisition quickly brought negotiations to a halt. When George found out, he was furious and for several weeks tried to resurrect discussions with the other company, all to no avail.

Yes, these two executives talked about their differences often, but they still seemed unable to avoid disasters like the two just mentioned. Both were owners, Karas owning 80 percent of the company and Martin and other senior executives owning the remaining 20 percent. This ownership situation made it both easier and more difficult to coordinate and integrate efforts.

Keeping What Works and Tossing What Fails

In an ideal world, I would have liked to counsel this company to strike a perfect balance between fastening and unfastening behavior. But this is not an ideal world. I have discovered over the years that different situations require more emphasis on one or the other rather than an equal, overall balance between the two. For example, organizations with intensive R&D requirements usually need to direct a fastening orientation outside while maintaining an unfastening one inside because they need creativity and innovation internally and structured and consistent marketing and sales externally.

In reality, OmniCare's George Karas felt more and more constrained and boxed in by Raymond Martin's fastening attitude, while at the same time Martin grew more and more frustrated with Karas's unfastening tendencies. Ultimately, the schism led to Martin's resignation and subsequent joining of a rival health care firm. It wasn't until after Raymond left the company that the chairman became more aware of what had caused the friction between his ex-president and himself. Eventually, he hired a new president, also a fastener, but not quite as unbending as his predecessor. The result was an environment that favored unfastening but allowed for fastening in between times of change. George's influence dominated the new relationship, thus creating the leaning toward unfastening; however, his experience with Raymond taught him to place greater value on the fastening orientation of his new COO.

Sometimes, blending fastening and unfastening traits works wonders; in other cases, it exacts great cost and pain. As with Omni-Care, attempting to equally balance the two often creates unproductive conflict. The inability on the part of the CEO and COO to truly value each others' perspectives brought about their eventual split. True valuing of both management and leadership orientations helps balanced and integrated organizations flourish, but even then, the natural tension between fastening and unfastening can quickly get out of hand when mutual respect falters.

27

Compromise plus Polarize

Managers Drive Toward Compromise; Leaders Work to Polarize

The manager's mind thinks *compromise*. In fact, most managers devote the majority of their time and attention to driving toward compromises in all aspects of organizing or directing the efforts of their groups and organizations. They constantly forge compromises with superiors, peers, and subordinates, making sure plans, programs, and policies get implemented. Compromising is a way of life for managers, because without it, the organization can quickly get caught in a gridlock of rising conflicts. Compromise reduces or eliminates conflict. "Let's iron out our differences," commands the manager.

The leader's soul seeks *polarization*. Most leaders spend their lives eliciting strong, diametrically opposed responses from superiors, peers, and subordinates. Polarization of viewpoints is a way of life for leaders because it flushes out the multiplicity of perspectives that enrich an undertaking. Polarization benefits an organization by weeding out people and ideas that don't fit the organization's particular culture or common purpose. "Let's find out where everyone really stands," implores the leader.

With a group of executives from a management services firm, I again witnessed how the tendencies to compromise or polarize can crash against one another. This particular firm, with many offices or project sites across the country, held long-term contracts with several large government and commercial organizations. The sixteen executives who comprised the corporate and project management team for the entire company had decided to hold a retreat in order to resolve some current sticky problems and plan for the future. During the process of dealing with these issues, the group divided on lines of compromise and polarization.

Polarizing

The CEO, Mark Teagan (a fictitious name), was an unusual combination of manager and leader who, in ten short years, had built the company from scratch into a $100 million operation. Teagan demanded a lot from his top management team, and he got it. However, some of the people with line responsibility for various contracts did not share his philosophy of operations nor his mix of management and leadership. This became clear during the second day of the retreat when a hotly debated issue regarding a future move toward project decentralization and autonomy turned into a free-for-all. Teagan adamantly opposed such a move because it would weaken the corporate culture and its continuity throughout the organization and across projects. Since centralized control and consistency had won the firm its great success, the CEO saw no reason to tamper with it. Some of the project executives, on the other hand, argued that each project was so unique that it made more sense to create and foster unique working environments and organizational cultures on a project-by-project basis. As conflict over this issue flared, I intervened with my own interpretation of it. If, I suggested, the CEO would not compromise on this issue, those project managers who couldn't accept the status quo should possibly reexamine whether they fit this corporate culture.

I then proposed further discussion, one on one, between the CEO and Robert Benton (not his real name), one of the more vocal project managers, later that evening. After dinner, Teagan and Benton spent several hours talking. Benton, unable to understand why the CEO would not consider decentralization, insisted that not doing so could really stall the company's future growth. Teagan argued that decentralization and autonomy would only serve to widen the disparity and unevenness among divisions just when consistency and standardization were the most important factors for the firm's landing and fulfilling federal government contracts. After much discussion, their positions polarized even further. Around 2:00 A.M., they tentatively agreed that Benton may want to transition out of the company over the next six months. A very compassionate man, Teagan vowed to help him find a top position with another firm.

In the end, Benton decided to stay with the company. Teagan maintained his centralized control, and Benton compromised his position but not his principles. Benton continued to believe he would eventually help the company become more decentralized in its approach to operations. While his position compromised, his principles became even more polarized precisely because of the compromise.

Compromising

Later that same week, I observed a less dramatic situation where the CEO, I thought, would have been smart to compromise. One of the firm's policies ruled against paying overtime to professional staff because the firm's culture demanded levels of commitment from these people that often required working longer than eight hours per day as part of their base salary. However, the firm had become one of several subcontractors on a ten-year airport renovation project where the lead management services group was paying overtime to its professional staff. Although other subcontractors happily accepted the overtime pay, an uncompromising Mark Teagan would not.

When this issue arose, Sara Joslyn, the project manager involved, suggested that the company allow an exception to this par- ·

ticular policy. It was causing resentment and wavering commitment among employees, who couldn't understand why the firm
would not allow them to receive overtime payments. However,
because Joslyn recognized the importance of the policy in maintaining high professional standards, she offered a compromise that
would allow the company to accept the overtime payments from
the prime contractor but hold them and pay them out to employees
as part of an incentive bonus program based on performance. Teagan
would not even accept this compromise and instructed Joslyn to refuse
any and all overtime pay offered by the prime contractor.

After the discussion, I sat down with Teagan to suggest that a
compromise on this issue would not damage the firm's policies and
culture, but enhance them. I felt that Sara Joslyn had displayed
unshakable commitment to the firm and its culture and was only
trying to respond to a unique situation. She wasn't asking for autonomy or decentralization or her own organizational culture. She
was asking for a minor adjustment to the firm's policy on overtime
pay. Despite my arguments, Teagan remained steadfastly opposed.
After the compromise was rejected, news of that fact had a paralyzing effect on Sara Joslyn and her team over the next several weeks,
with many employees thinking about defecting to other subcon-
tracting firms on the project.

Ironically, the prime contractor later compromised its position
by eliminating overtime pay to all subcontractors for the same reasons that Teagan had originally refused it. Teagan's polarization,
even though he was beginning to consider a compromise, actually
helped cause the prime contractor to compromise its position.

Knowing When to Compromise and When to Polarize

There is a time for iron-willed polarizing, and there is a time for
flexible compromising. If you only know how to compromise, you
miss the tonic effect of polarizing; if you only know how to polarize,
you miss those opportunities where a little bending could save the
day. But how do you know when to polarize and when to compromise? In the preceding case, the effects of polarizing and compro-

mising could not have been easily predicted. Consequently, leaders should continue polarizing, and managers should continue compromising — but be ready for the often unexpected results that come when polarizing and compromising are blended together. Compromise often fuels polarization and polarization often leads to compromise. The balanced and integrated organization uses this knowledge of compromise and polarization to bring about successful and lasting change.

28

Complexity plus Simplicity

Managers See Complexity; Leaders See Simplicity

When looking at internal and external situations, managers tend to see *complexity*. When attempting to see the full picture or understand the complete story behind a situation, the manager's mind turns to details, digging for data that may not be readily apparent. Given this inclination, managers, by and large, create rather complex perceptions of reality that contain all the details they can muster.

When leaders want to view the full picture, they do so by *simplifying*. The leader's soul searches for patterns, connections, frameworks, or concepts that encompass all the confusing details surrounding a situation. With this inclination, leaders create simple perceptions of reality. This doesn't mean that leaders see fewer details than managers — they probably see the same amount — but leaders use the details to find patterns and frameworks in order to simplify the complexity. Managers, on the other hand, use the details to paint the most realistic picture possible, with all its complexity.

A number of years ago I undertook some strategic planning work for a large conglomerate that was in the process of passing the reins of CEO to the next generation. The current CEO, a real entrepreneur I'll call Rader, had built the company largely through acquisitions. He now wanted to pass the power on to a more professional manager who could solidify the company and develop its future. The heir-apparent, I'll call him Dolan, was a man with the reputation of a consummate professional manager, having spent his early years with a well-known consulting firm and his more recent career as a senior executive with a widely admired, well-established company that prided itself on its professional management. Rader, having built a $2 billion company by being opportunistic and responsive to gut feelings, taking chances, and letting his acquisitions run themselves, realized that the company now needed to consolidate and solidify its many different profit centers and divisions. To do so, he had hired Dolan away from another company, where he had been serving as division president and CEO. Appreciating the magnitude of change his new company faced, Dolan hired a number of consultants including myself to team up with internal staff executives to hammer out the necessary strategic plan. The engagement went surprisingly smoothly until Rader ran in from the sidelines, where he had been observing us with mounting exasperation.

The Professional Manager's Agenda

Dolan, expecting soon to become the CEO, had invested heavily in the new strategic analysis and planning effort, which would analyze the current business base and propose alternatives for growth, acquisition, and divestiture. More than once he commented on the complexity of the task. Hoping to learn everything there was to know about the strengths of existing businesses in their particular industries, market trends, competitors, growth industries for the future, companies with enormous potential, and so on, Dolan wanted complete and precise data on all the different options. He assumed that only by fully understanding the complexity of the circumstances surrounding each of the company's businesses, the futures of other industries and markets, and all candidates for divestiture or acquisition could he chart a successful future for the company.

The Entrepreneurial Leader's Agenda

From the outset, Rader disdained this search for complexity. However, since he recognized that the company needed more professional managing in the future, he went along with our indepth analysis and planning, at least outwardly. I can vividly remember him talking at one meeting about the importance of blending the entrepreneurial with the professional, while Dolan nodded his head in approval. On the surface, the two executives seemed to value each other's orientation and saw a combination of the two operating in the future. However, over the course of our long, drawn-out effort, their inner feelings rose to the surface.

As Rader became more obviously impatient and frustrated, Dolan expressed more and more concern about Rader's stability, worrying aloud that he might do something rash in a moment of entrepreneurial zeal.

Finally, we wrapped up the strategic analysis and presented our painstakingly detailed and sophisticated report to the two men in a formal meeting. We covered every topic from environmental and market analysis, to strengths and weaknesses assessment, to competitive advantage projections, to strategic alternatives and recommendations. At one point, Rader remarked that all this effort seemed to him "a laborious and long way around the barn when the conclusion is obvious—we need to get rid of some businesses and acquire some others." Dolan rolled his eyes at these words. It wasn't that the CEO's comment was wrong, it wasn't. It simply lacked the precision that Dolan felt the company needed to move ahead.

The Best Laid Plans

For all the rhetoric about combining professional management with entrepreneurial leadership, these two individuals were so entrenched in their own particular orientations that neither could embrace the other's viewpoint except in words. I believe they genuinely wanted to value each other's orientations, as evidenced by their association in the first place. But when the talking and discussing ended and decisions had to be made, they held to their comfortable and predominant views. However, when, as part of the new strategic plan, the company made one particularly good $300 million acquisition, Rader seemed to calm down, feeling, perhaps, that the acquisition represented an entrepreneurial move by Dolan. By the same token, Dolan appeared to think that Rader had come around to a better appreciation of professional management. However, shortly after the acquisition, a battle royal erupted between the two men.

Rader got it into his head to merge with a company twice his own company's size, a move that would put him atop one of the largest corporations in America. Dolan violently opposed the merger on the grounds that it ran counter to all our complex analysis and planning and his own vision for the future of the company. When Rader continued his pursuit of this merger, the gap widened between him and Dolan. Then, on the eve of the merger, Dolan left for Europe for two weeks without telling anyone in the company where he was going. He had lost the battle. After returning from abroad, he resigned, and Rader, who became vice chairman of the board of the new company, toasted his own finest hour.

Unfortunately, the merger didn't last. As Dolan had suspected, the companies were not well suited to each other, their cultures clashed, and the anticipated business synergies never developed. After several years, the two companies split apart, with Rader's firm never fully recovering from the divorce. Pieces of it were sold off or acquired through management buy-outs. By this time, Rader had passed away, and Dolan was running another company.

In retrospect, I place most of the blame for this failure on the CEO, Rader, because I feel the COO, Dolan, really did try to imbue his professional management with an entrepreneurial spirit. In contrast, even though the CEO talked about the importance of professional management, he never really believed what he said. In cases of complexity versus simplicity, it may be easier for the manager to embrace some or part of the orientation of the leader than for the leader to assume some or part of the orientation of the manager. Everything looked simple to the CEO: If you wanted to do a merger that looked good, and the parties were willing, you did it. The COO, on the other hand, saw a more complex picture, recognizing from the beginning that the merger could spell disaster.

From my point of view, most organizations should look for complexity first and then find ways to simplify that complexity. Both orientations are critically important, but simplicity alone carries much more risk and potential for waste and inefficiency in an increasingly global and complex world. However, complexity in and of itself can fail because it obscures simple strategic priorities and cultural values that need to be clearly and easily communicated to people throughout the organization. In a balanced and integrated organization, managers work to bring the full picture with all its complexity into focus, while leaders complement their efforts by taking that complex picture and finding simple patterns and frameworks to make it easy to use and communicate.

29

Reaction plus Proaction

Managers React; Leaders Proact

Both managers and leaders respond to change, but in inherently different ways. The manager's mind preoccupies itself with change that has already happened or is currently occurring. Managers feel most comfortable in a defensive, "after the fact," rather than an offensive, "before the fact" posture, justifying such behavior by pointing out the folly of acting prematurely in any situation. Change is not real until it happens, then managers *react* to it.

The leader's soul consumes itself with anticipating or creating change. Generally taking the offensive, leaders *proact* in an effort to make change happen. They don't mind taking action before it becomes necessary. In fact, they'd rather force changes than let circumstances thrust changes on them. Even distant change is real for leaders because they are constantly trying to anticipate it.

A fascinating example of this difference between managers and leaders occurred in a large construction products manufacturing firm I'll call Willard-Cole. Willard-Cole's executives had concluded that the world market for cement and other materials used in the construction industry had become so globalized, with major international firms buying up companies around the world, that it could do nothing but wait to be gobbled up itself. I became involved with this company through the vice president of corporate planning and development, Don Knowlston (not his real name), who figured he needed an outside agent of change to get the company to take charge of its own destiny. As Don described it, "I seem to be the only member of the executive team concerned about really creating our own future."

The Fortress Mentality

The senior executives of this organization were more management-oriented than leadership-oriented, which was not surprising given the industry's and Willard-Cole's histories. While Willard-Cole was in the midst of a transition at the top from an old-guard CEO to a slightly more forward-thinking one, it could not easily overcome years and years of defensive posturing, nor could the CEO's heir-apparent. Through its investment bankers, the publicly held Willard-Cole had communicated to the *Wall Street Journal* that the firm was for sale. Two families controlled a sizeable portion of the stock and had decided to sell. When the *Journal* article came out, the company, management and owners alike, sat back to wait for a suitor to call. During this period, management did little but defend the fortress, containing costs, minimizing capital expenditures, and otherwise retaining, so they thought, as much of the firm's attractiveness to suitors as possible. Management began to rationalize its reactive response as the only thing it could do. Characteristic of this orientation, management became very defensive about its reactive posture.

On the Attack

In the midst of this "fortressing," I participated in the company's annual management conference at the request of Knowlston, who expected me to inspire the group to take a more proactive strategic approach to the future. He understood the danger of letting the industry changes run roughshod over the company. And regardless of whether the company would be sold or not, it was time to turn industry changes to Willard-Cole's advantage by being more strategically proactive and creative. In my talk to the group, I pointed out how companies in other industries had abandoned their fortresses and gone on the attack, not waiting for the future to arrive. By embarking on their own creative affiliations, joint ventures, mergers, and acquisitions, they had put their futures more in their own hands. Don loved this message and continued to preach it within the company. However, for most of the other members of the senior management team, the message fell on deaf ears. They truly believed that their reactive response would create the future.

Discretion and Valor

Sometimes it pays to act valiantly, other times you'd be wise to exercise a little discretion. There is a time to act and a time to react. Beware of getting so wrapped up in one response or the other that you can't adjust to the times. Unfortunately, Willard-Cole had set its responses in concrete. Within a year after the annual meeting, Don Knowlston was let go. The company, still waiting for something to happen, continues wallowing in marginal performance. Maybe the reactive posture will pay off, but I doubt it, because management has begun to sacrifice much of the company's attractiveness through inaction. Like most companies, Willard-Cole needed both reactive and proactive thinking within the executive group, but it fired its only source of the latter. This put Willard-Cole into a blindly reactive mode. As a result, morale in the company has declined, and many observers express doubts about whether the company can survive beyond the next two or three years.

It is by no means unusual for companies and executives today to talk about the need for a proactive as well as a reactive orientation. In fact, we have manufactured the right rhetoric for talking about change. However, we lack a deeper understanding of the differences in perspectives that unconsciously shape our individual and collective responses to change. Curiously, our rhetoric masks the reality that the manager's mind thinks *react* and the leader's soul feels *proact*. These thoughts and feelings will war with each other until we recognize and value the role of each in our organizations.

30

Plans
plus
Experiments

Managers Plan; Leaders Experiment

When organizations move in new directions or prepare for any sort of change, their managers get busy *planning*. Convinced that planning will minimize risk and maximize the chances for success, managers use their plans as road maps for the new course of action or the response to change. If done properly, managers argue, planning can help you foresee and forestall many problems.

Leaders would rather *experiment* with different scenarios, actually testing them out beforehand to ensure their workability. As a rule, leaders downplay the planning process because no matter how many problems your plans let you foresee, unanticipated events always occur. Experimentation, leaders believe, can smoke out such events.

My work with a small but rapidly emerging bank taught me a lot about the choice between planning and experimenting. The president of the bank, whom I'll refer to as Peter Wilson, was a manager by preference and training. He had come out of a very large banking environment that had heavily emphasized the careful planning of new courses of action. However, Wilson recognized that his new position would require a more entrepreneurial approach. He had been especially impressed by a McKinsey & Company white paper on the future of the financial services industry. It suggested that in the future, small, emerging banks would need to find new ways to serve newly identified niches in the marketplace.

Priding himself on his ability to keep current in his industry, Wilson had studied the McKinsey report and had discussed it with executives at other small, emerging banks. In essence, he debated the relative merits of developing an elaborate strategic plan to move into particular market niches that appear to be attractive, underserved, and potentially profitable or embarking on some experimentation with different services, products, and ways of doing business to test out their viability. On the one hand, the elaborate strategic plan alternative would offer a much more detailed analysis of market opportunities and possibly improve decision making and reduce risk. On the other hand, as one of his vice presidents often reminded him, the experimentation alternative would offer actual hands-on experience with different approaches and markets that might also improve decision making and reduce risk.

The Planning Mode

One particular underserved market niche seemed very attractive to Wilson because the bank had already begun serving customers in it and could very likely build on that base if it really tried. The niche Wilson had in mind was wealthy professionals and business owners. The bank had very successfully catered to this clientele, and no other bank seemed to be focusing specifically on its needs.

If the bank properly planned to gain a dominant position in this niche, it appeared that it could sustain this advantage for many years. Given Wilson's predilection toward planning in his prior job, he had already conducted several analyses to determine the viability of the niche and the bank's strengths in serving it. This all occurred before I became involved in the situation.

I remember one conversation with Peter Wilson in which he said, "You know, at my former company, we would have conducted a lot more analysis, even though the situation looks very attractive based on initial investigation." But for some reason, Wilson felt a need to listen to his outspoken vice president who had a leader's entrepreneurial flair. After all, a desire to exercise more entrepreneurial leadership had attracted him from the large banking environment to this small opportunity in the first place. To do so he would have to tap the energy and talent of those with more leadership orientation than he had. At this juncture, he just wasn't ready to bet the bank's future on strategic analysis and planning alone, even though his prior experience and personal orientation argued that he should.

The Experimentation Mode

Peter Wilson decided to experiment with and test the plan before totally committing the bank to it. I thought that this made especially good sense now that the ground work had been laid with some good preliminary analysis and many of the other potential strategies and market niche targets had been worked out. I complimented Wilson on his balanced approach and urged him to experiment freely.

Together, we worked out an approach whereby just one of the bank's five branches would focus completely on serving the upscale market niche identified by the planning process. Over a period of six to twelve months, this branch would focus on developing business almost exclusively in this niche and attempt to position itself as a dominant force. Drawing on the completed planning and analysis data, we applied the approach to this branch, with special attention to monitoring the results in terms of customer reaction.

The experiment began, and eight months later we could draw an important conclusion: Total focus on this one market niche had caused real problems in the branch. Customers simply would not switch banks as rapidly as Wilson had hoped or planned. Worse, some of the branch's customers who did not fit into the new niche felt the bank did not appreciate them and took their business elsewhere. On the bright side, the branch had made some inroads, slowly but surely, into the niche and had attracted several customers from other banks. All in all, Wilson felt he had learned a lot from the experiment—specifically, that neither planning alone nor experimenting alone provides the single key to optimal strategic decisions.

Plans that Incorporate Experiments

Organizations need to incorporate more experimenting into their planning process. In this particular case, the bank gained great benefit from the planning and analysis it conducted prior to actually attacking the target niche. Experimentation taught it something planning could never have anticipated—targeting the one market niche would probably too narrowly focus the bank in the short term. Instead, the bank should continue to target its niche, but broaden it slightly to include other related niches in which the bank could achieve a combined dominant position. Two related niches Wilson considered adding to his bank's targeted focus were beginning professionals that were not yet wealthy but potentially would be, and small businesses in general rather than just small business owners. This would allow the bank to focus on an expanded market base while incorporating important customers that formed part of the bank's current customer base. The bank went on to conduct some additional analysis and planning to identify related market niches and then followed up with another round of experimentation. In the end, the bank developed a successful strategy, targeting a related group of market niches that secured its reputation as one of the most rapidly growing and most profitable banks in the region.

Planning alone is not enough, and experimentation alone is not enough. An organization needs both, or else it may make the mistake of either beating itself with willy-nilly experimenting or paralyzing itself with exhaustive planning. I'm not the first to say this, of course. Most businesspeople today are acutely aware of this issue. However, few organizations have perfected the process of intertwining planning and experimenting into one iterative process. Of course, many companies engage in test marketing before launching a full marketing campaign, but the blending together of planning and experimenting at several points in the process still eludes them. Plan some, then experiment some, then plan some more, and then experiment some more, so that planning and experimenting stop being two different processes, but become elements of a single integrated process. This makes especially good sense in an age when time to market represents such a major success factor for most organizations.

31

Reorganize plus Rethink

Managers Reorganize; Leaders Rethink

When faced with change, managers see a need to *reorganize* things because, to their way of thinking, reorganization will better prepare people to handle the change. Reorganization does give people a course of action to pursue in responding to change. Despite the fact that this often makes sense, however, it sometimes simply moves things around and doesn't address the real needs created by external or internal change.

In the same situation, leaders see change as an opportunity to *rethink* what's going on inside and outside the organization. While their rethinking may lead to reorganization, it involves much more than this because leaders want to get at real needs, and this means digging beneath the surface. This usually takes more time, and sometimes the organization must move quickly to adapt to change and therefore may not enjoy the luxury of rethinking. However, leaders would answer that every organization, no matter what the circumstances, must take time to rethink.

While consulting with a group of eleven senior managers from a diversified service company, I once again saw the tension between reorganizing and rethinking play itself out as we wrestled with the issue of responding to changes and opportunities in this particular company's markets. The company owned and operated several different service businesses, including a cable TV company, an equipment rental company, a lawn and yard care company, and a construction company.

The First Day: Reorganization

At the helm of this company stood Ben Hill (not his real name), a CEO with very specific ideas about responding to changes in the external market by reorganizing internally. The company was growing fast. There were market opportunities to pursue, internal synergies to capture, and acquisitions to make. Even before the retreat, Hill had convinced himself that a complete reorganization of the company would best protect its future. However, since he wanted the support of his management team, he figured he could use the retreat to persuade everyone to accept his view. During the entire first day, we talked about various configurations of reorganization. As the day wore on, some members of the management group became more and more frustrated with the limited view that only reorganization could pave the way to greater growth and profitability. By about four o'clock on the first day, it seemed we had accomplished very little. No clear reorganization plan had emerged, and the chief financial officer, Gene Kroll, who had urged a deeper rethinking, had become very outspoken in his concern that the group should change its approach entirely. Kroll felt that the company's almost random pursuit of new markets and acquisitions was becoming a big problem and that it should take a new look at business groupings and combinations. The best way to go about this, he urged, was to rethink everything about the company's business and its future growth prospects, as well as potential acquisitions.

At the end of the day, I set the agenda aside, encouraging everyone to speak openly about his or her feelings about the day's activities. As individuals tried to put their confusion and frustration into words, it became clear that a fundamental schism existed in the group between those who inclined toward the CEO's position and those who agreed more with the CFO, who summed up his feelings by saying, "We have been so preoccupied with reorganizing things that we haven't stopped to rethink what we're really doing." I met privately with Ben Hill that evening and convinced him to let me take a different approach the following day.

The Second Day: Rethinking

As we began the second day, I asked Gene Kroll to take the lead and help the group seriously rethink the company's priorities, its strategic positions, its policies, its intercompany relationships, its acquisition plans, and every other basic issue that could influence its future. He did so by asking the group to identify the major, most critical issues the company faced. The prior day's experience had prompted some to start digging more deeply even before the session began, so we quickly progressed beneath the surface of reorganization. As the second day unfolded, even Ben Hill reluctantly recognized the value of the discussion, and at one point he even apologized for having taken too narrow a view the day before. This really opened things up.

By the end of the day, we had delved into a number of critical issues that could strongly influence the current and future operations of the company. However, the management group concluded that it should not make any firm decisions at this point but should, instead, gather and analyze more data prior to another meeting a month hence.

Rethink First; Reorganize Second

When we got together again a month later, the management team made some key decisions about the future of the company, which included repositioning itself in the marketplace by stressing quality of service in each of the businesses. This would become a uniting strategic focus for all the companies, where there had been no such unity before. The team also designed business groups that could gain synergies between companies. For example, one group linked the cable TV and construction companies together, with plans to add a landscaping firm to the group as well as an interior design and remodeling firm. All this came about as a direct result of rethinking everything from the ground up. In the end, the company gained a new lease on life and, yes, reorganized itself to a large degree. However, the reorganization did not follow the plan that Ben Hill had originally designed prior to the retreat, a plan that called for centralization of marketing for all the companies in order to gain needed synergies. This quick-fix reorganization would probably not have accomplished much, because it treated symptoms, not causes.

In situations that revolve around anticipating or creating change, you should probably rethink before you reorganize. By rethinking first, you can make sure that any reorganizing does more than superficially appease anxiety about the future.

Sometime later I visited with Ben Hill to find out what had happened since the retreat. With a grin, he explained that the changes the company had made as a result of its rethinking effort had turned out better than anticipated, with both growth and profits well ahead of initial projections. The business groupings had brought new clarity and focus to the marketing and sales functions, and the company was now looking for additional ways to improve its operations and quality of service. Hill felt that he had learned an important lesson, namely, to curb his impulse to reorganize until he had done some deeper rethinking beforehand. "Whenever I feel that old urge to move things around, I have lunch with Gene Kroll. He always has a bucket of cold water handy."

In balanced and integrated organizations, managers and leaders blend their orientations but sometimes one orientation guides the other. In the case of rethinking and reorganizing, the former usually takes precedence.

32

Refine plus Revolutionize

Managers Refine; Leaders Revolutionize

Given their preference for stability, managers tend to look for ways to *refine* existing aspects of an organization. For the manager, such polishing and fine-tuning represents the most cost-effective approach, since it builds on existing positions and poses few obvious risks. The mind of the manager considers refinement the ultimate state of corporate well-being because it implies a solid foundation, good systems, and strong positions. To the manager, revolutionary change is coarse and unnecessary for the well-run organization.

The leader, impatient with small, incremental improvements, would far rather *revolutionize* aspects of an organization. For leaders, refinement presents the riskier course because it fails to take advantage of the up-side potential of great change. The soul of the leader identifies revolutionary change as the real test of an organization's strength. Only through such change can you search for new horizons. Refinement represents stagnation, fear of change, and perpetuation of the past.

The difference between these two outlooks became readily apparent at an international marketing symposium where I delivered the keynote speech. During the conference, I met and talked with several CEOs, both in formal workshop settings and in informal discussions over meals. Norway, the host country, had been struggling for years to add sufficient value to its natural resources to turn the country's economy around. In the past, it had merely shipped its raw materials and natural resources out of the country, thus allowing companies in other countries to add the value and then send them back as imports. Most of the companies in Norway had approached this problem by continuing to increase their exports of raw materials and natural resources, but in more cost-effective, higher-volume ways. In other words, refinement summed up their basic approach to the dynamic changes in the global marketplace. However, one company that had taken a revolutionary approach to this problem was reaping huge profits.

The Refining Mentality

The owners and managers of some of Norway's fish-processing companies best represented the refinement mentality. An abundance of commercial fish in the waters offshore had caused a number of companies to grow up over time. Their ships would catch fish and then ship them to other countries with little or no processing beforehand. Companies in other countries would then process the fish into canned and frozen food and other commercial products. When the global market for fish began heating up, these fishing companies felt enormous pressure to find ways to compete and survive. Their response? Catch more fish. To do so, they increased the size of their fleets, improved the technology for catching fish, and kept costs in line by doing as little processing as possible. So bent were they on refining the old ways of doing things that they failed to recognize the opportunities they could gain by adding more value at home, i.e., processing more fish before sending them out of the country. The majority of the fishing industry executives who attended the symposium reflected this refining mentality.

The Revolutionizing Spirit

One head of a small business who attended the conference, however, had been behaving like a leader. A fisherman and sailor from birth and by training, he somehow had developed a revolutionary spirit that could appreciate how adding more value at home could make his country more of a global competitor. Instead of minimally processing the fish he caught and sending them off to other countries, this fellow had set about finding a way to package the fish more completely at home. Tapping family trusts and savings and using investments from a handful of adventuresome friends, he began packaging his fish with exotic sauces and selling them as delicacies. Interestingly, many of his recipes for pickling fish were centuries old and considered Norwegian treasures. But no one else in Norway, certainly no fishing industry executive, had ever thought of marketing such products to the world. By adding processing value, this leader not only turned a handsome profit, but he contributed to the world's respect for his country's culture. Before long, he was selling his products to luxury ships cruising the area, to airlines, to hotels, and to an increasing number of distributors outside the country. Eventually, the company began selling its products in grocery stores both in neighboring and distant countries with great success. Clearly, the revolutionary spirit had outdistanced the refinement mentality.

Avoiding Myopic Mind-Sets or Soul-Sets

Sometimes refining the existing way of doing things provides the perfect answer to the problem of adapting to change. For example, once a company has positioned itself effectively after a major industry change or market revolution, it may be best to pursue a refinement path. If the environment has been saturated with change, refinement can increase profits. At other times, however, refining old ways ignores opportunities and fails to utilize changing environments and circumstances to advantage. For example, long periods of only minor or refining change, internal or external, brings about entrenchment. At this point, revolutionary change can be very appropriate. The trick, in either case, is to avoid allowing either mind-set or soul-set to become myopic, blinding you and your organization to the need for the other mentality at given times. This is not easy, because while many managers and leaders articulate the need both to refine and to revolutionize, their unconscious emotional and psychological makeup causes them to set their minds and souls inadvertently.

At the end of the marketing symposium, I summed up my observations on this particular issue by suggesting that people in companies today must unite their varied perspectives and strengths to effectively develop the most viable and timely course of action. Managers who prefer the refining path should unite with leaders to consider revolutionary courses of action whenever their refinements fail to create success in the global economy. And leaders oriented toward revolutionizing should unite with managers to focus more on necessary refinements when such a course is essential to optimum development of the company. Both mentalities, I stressed, are sorely needed in the face of the increased global competitiveness and change we will experience in the 1990s.

V

Individual Effectiveness/ Style

As organizations become more effective and efficient, rising to amazing heights, they will owe the achievement to individuals who have themselves attained peak performances. Individual performance, more than anything else, will fuel balanced and integrated organizations and will do so with a rich array of styles. With respect to individual effectiveness and style, managers and leaders naturally diverge. Here more than in any other area managers and leaders will find it hard both to appreciate their differences and to integrate them. Management-dominated organizations will find it hard to add unstructured approaches and processes to their formal ones. By the same token, leadership-driven organizations will have trouble adding structured approaches and processes to their unstructured, spontaneous, and loose ones. Conflict-oriented organizations will find it difficult to stop pitting more structure against less structure, and vacillation-prone organizations will have a hard time overcoming their inconsistency. Success for each will hinge on its ability to integrate the mind of the manager with the soul of the leader into a unified whole that can become much more than the sum of its parts.

In this section you will see how differences in effectiveness and style create tough problems for organizations and individuals, and you will watch as, inevitably, the best long-term solutions to problems come from tapping the natural tension between leaders and managers.

33

Methods
plus
Motives

Managers Ask How; Leaders Wonder Why

Methods, that is, *how* you go about doing something, preoccupy most managers, who feel that organizational or personal motives don't matter much as long as you know what to do and how to do it. Managers usually subscribe to an "Ours is not to reason why" philosophy, which places great emphasis on the "how to" side of business activities.

In contrast, leaders do worry about motives, that is, *why* you want to do something in the first place, because they feel that the reasons behind your decisions and actions make all the difference in the world. Their philosophy hinges on the notion, "Only do what's worth doing."

One executive vice president (EVP) of a Fortune 500 firm with whom I have worked displayed deep devotion to understanding and communicating the "whys" of corporate objectives, policies, and programs. Having been brought in from outside the company, however, he was experiencing a great deal of frustration because the executives who reported to him seemed totally incapable of or disinterested in asking such questions. To help solve this problem, this executive asked me to join him in developing a corporate staff planning process that would ensure that all the over 1000 corporate staff personnel attended to both the "whys" and "hows" of their jobs and the company's mission. Determined to include business planning as one of the company's key areas of distinctive competence, this executive felt strongly that long-term success depended on emphasizing both motives and methods. It had to start, of course, at the corporate staff level.

When Too Much "How" Compromises the Future

On one occasion, the EVP had asked his vice president of corporate planning and financial analysis to initiate a plan for better integration of financial and marketing analysis, a key, he thought, to making business planning one of the firm's greatest strengths. During a brief meeting the EVP outlined his request. When several weeks elapsed with no action, the EVP went to the corporate planning vice president for an update. As it turned out, the corporate planning vice president had, in fact, sketched out the basics of a plan, which he happily handed to the EVP. Immediately, the EVP began asking "why" questions, and within a few minutes, he realized that the corporate planning vice president had not thought about those issues but had simply responded to the EVP's initial request by concocting a somewhat cursory planning methodology. "How" had overruled any consideration of "why." As the two executives talked, the EVP became more and more upset, despairing that they'd never accomplish improved integrated planning without everyone understanding why it was so vital to the company's future. For him, without understanding why improved business planning was so important, no planning process would ever work. People would just go through the motions. Going through the motions, obviously, would not enhance effectiveness, productivity, or the bottom line.

Coincidentally, I came walking down the hall to the EVP's suite when I saw him storm out of the corporate planning vice president's office and slam the door behind him. After he cooled down a bit, we chatted about the incident. The EVP confided that he had lost his temper, but he still felt angry over the corporate planning vice president's unwillingness to ask the "whys." He lamented, "Can't he see that his approach is compromising our future, not to mention my view of his competence and effectiveness? This guy is just sleep-walking, he refuses to think."

When Overemphasis on "Why" Immobilizes the Present

As in most organizations, news of the door slamming incident traveled quickly through corporate headquarters. (I had not been the only witness in the executive suite corridor at the time.) One executive, the director of strategic analysis and acquisitions, who reported to the corporate planning vice president, thought he got the message and began asking "whys." In fact, he began riding his staff to make sure they knew exactly why they were doing what they were doing before they did it, to the point that it immobilized the entire group for almost a month, at which time other departments interacting with his department began to complain. His fear of the EVP's "hot" button caused a severe overreaction.

When the director's boss, the corporate planning vice president, called him on the carpet, he justified his behavior as consistent with the EVP's philosophy. "Hey, we're just taking the time to answer the 'whys,' before we jump into anything!" When the corporate planning vice president told him he had gone overboard, he defended himself by insisting that his boss was not paying attention to the EVP's philosophy. Later, I interviewed both these executives and passed my assessment on to the EVP, saying basically that he should schedule a meeting with key corporate staff managers in order to spell out his expectations, to get feedback, and to discuss how to proceed for mutual benefit.

Methods plus Motives Help
Balance the Future with the Present

Soon thereafter, the EVP did hold a two-day corporate staff management meeting at which he delivered one of the most eloquent speeches I've ever heard on the importance of people knowing both the "whys" and "hows" of their jobs in forging a great corporation. He discussed how focusing on only the "why" can create an abstract environment devoid of action, and how focusing only on the "how" can create an active but unthinking state. "We need both," he said, "and we need them simultaneously." He described the optimal environment for maximized individual effectiveness: one that continually asks and answers the questions *"Why* are we doing what we are doing?" and *"How* are we doing the things we have chosen to do?" He then stated that the company currently focused too much on the "how," giving various examples to illustrate his point. One of the examples illustrated how one executive, assigned to make improvements in the planning process, had proceeded with the assignment without really understanding or appreciating why he was doing it. He was simply fulfilling an assignment. The EVP challenged everyone never to feel satisfied until "you know exactly why you are doing what you're doing." He also committed himself to giving better explanations and encouraging more discussions of the "whys" behind objectives, policies, programs, assignments, and priorities.

During the rest of the meeting, discussion groups and workshops were organized to spell out exactly what it means to focus simultaneously on methods and motives when planning for the future and performing in the present. For those who participated, the meeting marked a major step toward resolving the EVP's concerns about his corporate staff and their attempts to develop an integrated business planning process.

When it comes to methods and motives, people need to question, understand, and communicate both. Leaders and managers must therefore work closely together in order to maintain an equilibrium. In the process, leaders will come to appreciate even more the importance of methods, while managers will come to value motives more highly.

34

Logical Thinking plus Lateral Thinking

Managers Think Logically; Leaders Think Laterally

This is not an either/or issue. Leaders can and do think logically, and managers can and do think laterally. However, each does exhibit a strong personal preference for the one or the other style of thought.

Logic implies sequential, linear, step-by-step thinking that leads to clearly structured, easily followed solutions. Lateral thinking, on the other hand, which zigzags and moves in a series of seemingly unconnected steps, leads to unpredictable and often surprising solutions. Managers' minds seem most comfortable with *logical thinking* and thus rely on it predominantly, further strengthening and entrenching their orientation. Leaders' souls seem to foster *lateral thinking*, which perpetuates itself as their first choice of thinking approaches. For example, a service-industry manager faced with a market-expansion decision might favor a logical extension such as an adaptation of an existing service to a new market, while a leader in the same situation might propose a lateral extension that would get the company into a brand new, but related, line of business. The former approach builds on strengths in a logical way; the latter draws on strengths in an unorthodox way.

I once worked with a client, I'll call him James Mallory, a division head at a large consumer products company, who had used lateral thinking to forge a remarkably successful career. He had been responsible for directing the strategic marketing affairs of a $300 million business at the age of twenty-six. Then, having traveled the fast track for several years, at the age of thirty-nine, he was now running a $700 million division of a Fortune 500 company. Within the company he had developed a reputation as a maverick, a reputation that clearly had not hurt him during his rapid rise to the top. He had taken unusual courses of action and associated risks that had brought extraordinary growth to the businesses in which he had become involved. In one case, he had almost single-handedly orchestrated the resurrection of a twenty-year-old wall decor product line that became a big winner, much to everyone's surprise.

Now, however, he had begun to suspect that his reputation was hurting him. His immediate supervisor, a group vice president, was a logically thinking manager, as was his superior, the chief operating officer. The group vice president didn't like what he considered odd-ball, strange, weird, or wild ideas, an attitude he made crystal clear to his subordinates. While the company had supposedly hired me to help the division clarify and further develop its strategic direction, in reality, I soon realized, it had invited me in to help Mallory communicate and sell his own strategic plan to his boss and the executive committee.

Lateral Thinking Runs Afoul of Logic

Mallory had created a vision of selling his division's products through a totally new channel of distribution, a concept that had naturally encountered strong resistance from top management. This division manufactured a wide range of houseware products and home repair tools, marketing them through department stores, hardware stores, and home improvement specialty outlets. Mallory had come up with the unusual idea, at the time, of marketing the division's products through supermarket chains. His boss viewed the strategy as not only illogical, but extremely risky. A more logical path for the division to follow would, he argued, involve the addition of new products and a new emphasis on home improvement outlets as an underemphasized and growing channel of distribution. Such moves represented a logical, sequential, and linear development of the business, easy to understand, easy to follow, and easy to explain to stockholders. Marketing through supermarkets represented an off-the-wall, unproven, and potentially dangerous idea. Not only would such a move alienate existing distribution channels, but it would fail to build on existing company positions. Despite this view from top management, Mallory remained steadfast in his belief that his strategy not only could work, but could generate enormous growth. Could I help him sell the concept to his bosses?

After spending many hours analyzing the division's current strategic position and the viability of a supermarket strategy, I came to appreciate Mallory's thinking. In fact, I concluded that if this division did not pursue the supermarket strategy, a competitor soon would and thus would capitalize on the benefits of being the first to pursue the new channel of distribution to sell an integrated line of housewares and home improvement products.

Lateral Thinking Uses Logic in Its Own Game

More than anything else, Mallory needed a way to communicate his laterally conceived strategy in a logical fashion. Because he tended to express his viewpoints adamantly and dogmatically, Mallory's arguments had not convinced his superiors. Acting as if he assumed any dolt should be able to grasp the concept immediately, Mallory had put off the more logical thinkers.

Together, Mallory and I hammered out a plan that would "fight fire with fire" by using the very tools of logic to put across the unconventional strategy. First, we tracked down and summarized seven examples of similar channel-of-distribution shifts in other industries. Interestingly, observers had often labeled these shifts risky and questionable before they finally began working. For example, many industry executives and observers suggested that the then new L'eggs pantyhose being sold in grocery stores would probably never take hold because women preferred buying their hosiery in department stores. After L'eggs became a great success and a trend-setter, the once suspect executives and observers became chagrined believers. In each case, the decision to move into a totally new channel of distribution seemed logical and clearly justifiable after the fact. In our own case, we needed to get that 20/20 hindsight into the foreground, placing Mallory's lateral thinking in a larger, longer-term, and thus more logical context.

We also took great pains to provide an objective analysis of up-side and down-side possibilities. All the possible risks, obstacles, and potential pitfalls were presented with an assessment of their probable impact. Likewise, all the possible benefits, advantages, and breakthrough opportunities were presented with an assessment of worst, best, and most likely cases. Not surprisingly, and rather logically, it took no fewer than five major presentation sessions to get top management's approval.

Almost immediately after the company launched the strategy, it began paying off dividends, both in sales and in the company's image as a pacesetter in the industry. The division enjoyed a very profitable leadership position in the supermarket channel of distribution for several years and continues to maintain a substantial market share.

Mallory left the company a few years after implementing the strategy to become CEO and a major shareholder of another company he and a group of investors purchased through a leveraged buy-out. He continues to think laterally, but now he knows how to communicate his surprising ideas more logically in order to build understanding and appreciation in others.

Communication Makes the Difference

In the situation I just described, we saw a lateral thinker attempting to communicate with logical thinkers, which generally poses more problems than the other way around. Still, even though logical thinking is, by definition, easier to follow and understand than lateral thinking, even the most logical thinker can fail to present his or her ideas effectively. In either case, the key to persuasion lies less in the realm of logic than in the realm of communication. In balanced and integrated organizations, both logical and lateral thinkers appreciate each other's style of thinking and attempt to communicate their ideas in a way that promotes understanding, appreciation, and superior decision making.

35

Hierarchy plus Equality

Managers Perpetuate Hierarchies; Leaders Strive for Equality

Managers by and large gain their identities and a sense of value from the *hierarchies* in which they work. Hierarchies provide structure, rationale, and order to an organization, all of which draw the mind of the manager. Thus managers perpetuate the hierarchies, making sure they apply to everyone in their organizations. If it took one manager ten years to move up two levels of management, then it should take about the same amount of time for another.

Leaders, who usually grow impatient with structure and order, strive to bring about *equality* in their organizations. They want people to progress and develop at their own pace, with equal chances for all. While leaders realize that not everyone will become equal in an organization, they still wish to provide equal opportunity for maximum growth and development. The leader's soul is drawn toward the idea that people move at their own pace and often achieve more than they themselves or others think they can.

A few years back I became involved with one of America's largest corporations, where the founder's son ran a key division. In the process of conducting several strategic development and culture-building sessions with this division president, whom I'll refer to as Don, I came to understand his deep respect for hierarchies, which he thought reflected the natural order of things. Adding to his inherent orientation, Don's father had raised him to believe that hierarchies brought order to an otherwise chaotic world and provided the best framework for performance. Within his own division worked an operations vice president, I'll call him Sam, who reported to Don and whom everyone assumed would eventually succeed Don as division president. However, I soon detected a major obstacle in Sam's path: He was a leader striving for equality in a environment of entrenched hierarchies. Sam liked to refer to everyone he worked with as associates and avoided giving too much attention to the organization's hierarchy. He did so because he wanted all the people in operations to feel equally committed to the division's performance and results.

Humanizing Hierarchies

During the course of my consulting sessions with this division, which included informal interviews and discussions squeezed between rather formal meetings, I observed an interesting phenomenon. While most people in the organization respected Don's strong hierarchical orientation, most also admired the way Sam eased the rigidity of the system by treating everyone more or less as equals. Sam made everyone feel that their individual contributions were just as vital and important as his to the success of the division. Everyone, he seemed to think, was important, and anyone could rise within the organization. From time to time, he had even suggested moving into new areas of business for the sole purpose of affording individuals new and wider opportunities for growth. Although Don continued to implement hierarchical mandates rigidly, issuing edicts and enforcing strict reporting relationships throughout the organization, people never found them unduly harsh or unreasonable because Sam would mold the mandates to individuals with an aura of "we're all in this together." Since so many of the people in the division reported to him, Sam could effectively provide the leavening of hierarchy required to keep people happy and fulfilled. For example, when Sam received an order to cut back on overtime hours, he gathered the full group of operations' personnel together (over 400 people) and discussed with them the need to contain costs for the well-being of the division. Cutting overtime hours was a sensitive issue, but Sam communicated the division's situation clearly and asked if anyone could come up with an alternative solution. His people responded to Sam's message by willingly cutting overtime hours and implementing several other cost-saving measures.

Realistic Equality

At the same time, I discovered another curious phenomenon: Don also had brought a leavening influence to bear on Sam. Without ever explicitly stating this goal, and perhaps without even understanding that he was achieving it, Don balanced Sam's preoccupation with equality with his own approach to hierarchy. Don felt strongly that not everyone in the organization could ever be equal. People at higher levels in the organization deserved higher salaries, expanded opportunities, and intensified development in accordance with their greater responsibilities, a reward that applied to whoever achieved those levels. Interestingly, Sam's belief in equality and Don's reliance on hierarchy brought about a general evenhandedness and equity within the organization. Together, they gave deference to a hierarchy in which people worked at different positions based on their performance, talents, abilities, and success in making things happen while at the same time maintaining opportunities for people to rise, develop, and grow. When Sam wanted to promote someone, Don would stand by certain hierarchical traditions within the division. As Sam tried to abide by these traditions in his own flexible way, the organization prospered.

An Unhappy Ending

As I concluded the strategy sessions with the division, I tried to articulate to Don what I had learned about the meshing of styles in his organization. However, the more I talked, the more baffled he looked. He did not seem to have much appreciation for what I was talking about. "Anyway, it doesn't matter," he concluded. "I'm moving on to a corporate management post; Sam will be taking over in a few months."

Hearing this, I said I feared that Sam could not maintain the current balance. Too great an emphasis on equality could, I felt, undermine the hierarchy of the division to the point that people would start feeling confused and frustrated. Well, to make a long story short, my argument fell on deaf ears. Both men were just too intent on moving up to their new positions to consider the consequences.

A little over two years later, Sam was fired from the company. From another division executive I found out the whole, sad story. When Sam became president and attempted to bring greater equality to the division by implementing new organizational structures and processes virtually devoid of any hierarchy, people had responded enthusiastically at first. Yet, slowly but surely, even key people began expressing confusion and anxiety. For example, one of Sam's first moves was do away with two levels of management by creating work groups with group leaders. When several people left the organization soon thereafter, Sam couldn't believe it. Here he was trying to create an organizational environment that would provide maximum opportunity, and people were turning their backs on it. Sam failed to recognize that the departing people just couldn't handle the confusion and frustration they felt in the new "no-hierarchy" environment. After the company let Sam go, it brought Don back to run the division once again, but now his hierarchical emphasis, with its rigid reporting relationships and strongly phrased mandates, lacked any leavening influence and ended up straitjacketing the organization. Now people began screaming that the pendulum had swung too far the other way. The division's performance plummeted, and rumors began circulating that the parent company would sell the division.

Sometimes people achieve a harmonious meshing of the manager's and leader's perspectives without really recognizing how or why they did so. This becomes especially disturbing when you want to recreate the blending in another situation, but can't figure out or appreciate how you did it the first time. When it comes to hierarchies and equality, a simple awareness of the dynamics between management and leadership and their inherent orientations can go a long way toward maintaining the right kind of empowering blend.

36

Skepticism
plus
Optimism

Managers Are Skeptical; Leaders Are Optimistic

In terms of personal style, managers tend to adopt a more generally *skeptical* stance than do leaders, who tend to express much more *optimism*. This occurs because the mind of the manager focuses on the down-side possibilities before the up-side possibilities, while the soul of the leader considers the up side before the down side. Since managers pride themselves on their objectivity and enjoy a reputation for cautious and deliberate business decisions, they naturally build a good deal of skepticism into their analyses of situations. Thus they seldom buy into a suggestion, plan, or alternative without playing "devil's advocate" for all the angles. Their natural skepticism causes them to appear less emotional, less passionate, and less able to make a leap of faith. This is not to say that managers cannot become passionately committed to causes, but rather that they tend to do so only after applying the test of skepticism.

However, leaders tend to feel keenly optimistic from the outset. Since their initial reactions to proposed strategies, alternatives, or ideas run in the direction of optimism, they often seem more immediately emotional and passionate about an idea. This natural optimism causes a leader to champion ideas or courses of action quite early in the game, while the manager is still playing critic. Of course, organizations need both champions and critics, although in different measures at different times.

I recently performed some work for a high-tech company, a developer and producer of measurement instruments and computer peripherals, that had developed a brilliant mix of championing and critiquing ideas and alternatives. In fact, the company explicitly weighs these traits when hiring or promoting key people.

The Champions

Because, like most high-tech companies, Saturn (a fictitious name) heavily depended on the development of new products, it needed to constantly fuel innovation and creativity. Innovation, Saturn felt, required leaders who could champion new ideas so they wouldn't get lost or fall between the cracks. To ensure this, the company actually institutionalized the development of champions.

When an employee came up with a new product idea or a scheme for modifying an existing product, that person sought out a sponsor from among Saturn's ten senior managers. At this stage, neither the innovator nor the executive encountered any serious hurdles they had to jump in order to pursue an idea. The employee merely needed to get an optimistic sponsor to marshall some planning, attention, and resources behind the idea. Of course, the company imposed some limits, such as 25 percent of an employee's or a group's time and not more than $10,000 in resources, initially.

At this point in the innovation process, optimism overruled all else. With little restraint, the organization encouraged ideas, made sponsors readily available, and stimulated every employee to get involved in some way with two, three, or four new product ideas or product modification projects. Those people naturally oriented toward skepticism were encouraged to unite with those more oriented toward optimism during this stage, allowing the optimists to take the lead. When it came to innovation and creativity, Saturn literally buzzed with activity. Obviously, this environment contributed greatly to the company's rapid growth over five years from $10 million to over $200 million in sales. Its approach had become a model for many others in its own and related industries, with competitors aggressively attempting to recruit Saturn's people.

The Critics

At the next stage of the innovation process, Saturn introduced skepticism into the process by requiring that every idea for a new or modified product undergo intense scrutiny and criticism before receiving additional investments of time and resources. In other words, if a new product idea had won sponsorship and had benefited from up to 25 percent of a person's or a group's time and up to $10,000 in resources, then the idea became the focus of skepticism, and not just by folks sitting on the sidelines, but by the innovators and the champions themselves. During this stage, the natural optimists were encouraged to combine with natural skeptics, allowing the skeptics to take the lead. Knowing what was expected from them at this point, both innovators and champions worked to make sure the critique of their idea was thorough and complete. Otherwise, they would not win additional time and resources for their ideas. I found it quite amazing to watch the champions and innovators draw on the orientations and perspectives of different people in shifting from optimistic to skeptical modes. The results proved the power of the "one plus one equals three" equation. Although fewer than 10 percent of all ideas survived the critiquing stage, the process encouraged so many ideas in the first stage that Saturn always enjoyed more new product opportunities than it could handle. No wonder it became the technological leader in most of the markets in which it competed.

Optimism **Before** *Skepticism,*
then Skepticism **Before** *Optimism*

Saturn understood the proper staging of optimism and skepticism. A company that relies heavily on innovation for its competitive advantage in the marketplace must develop both traits, but instead of allowing one to undermine the other, it should use one to strengthen the other. In Saturn's case, a product idea may make it past the intense skeptical stage and then shift back into an optimistic mode only to experience another shift back to skepticism before it actually moves into full production. At this stage, critiquing becomes even more arduous and rigorous to ensure that no products reach the marketplace without every assumption having been tested and retested.

One example of a product that moved through these stages was a template for improving the effectiveness and productivity of a personal computer's mouse device. At first, the idea was heralded as a breakthrough and given great encouragement. With a sponsor identified, the employee with the idea was able to quickly assemble a team that would put some meat on the bones of this idea. The team spent approximately 20 to 25 percent of its time over a three-month period developing the idea and only spent a little over $7000 before the concept was ready to move to the next stage. The team, adding a few appropriate members to ensure balance through the process, turned ruthless in its scrutiny of the template and its viability as a commercial venture. Prototypes were demonstrated to potential customers to obtain feedback. Sales and production forecasts were developed with an eye toward the down-side potential and the worst-case scenario.

After a lot of skeptical analysis, the template looked like a winner and was scheduled for test marketing in five selected geographic areas and with three large computer manufacturers. The template idea had made it and was now moved into another optimistic stage. However, it would face another skeptical stage after test marketing and before an international product introduction campaign.

Whether you are a manager or a leader, knowing when to shift the emphasis of a group or organization from optimism to skepticism and back again provides one key to organizational success, particularly in an age that demands constant renewal.

37

Smoothing plus Confronting

Managers Smooth; Leaders Confront

Obviously, both managers and leaders find themselves in confrontive and nonconfrontive situations, but their natural tendencies lead most leaders to prefer *confronting* people, issues, and problems, while most managers would rather try to *smooth things over* in order to prevent wasteful debate or discussion. The soul of the leader likes to address matters head-on. The mind of the manager acts more indirectly, in an effort to avoid potentially volatile confrontations. With confrontation, the leader hopes to clarify where people stand in order to build commitment and unity. "Let's get this issue out on the table and address it so we can move forward," urges the leader. At the same time, managers would rather avoid time-consuming disputes. "Let's handle this situation smoothly," managers say, "so it doesn't disrupt business."

Over the years, my dealings with consultants in such firms as McKinsey & Company, Booz Allen, Boston Consulting Group, Bain & Company, Ernst & Young, Price Waterhouse, and others have taught me a lot about these two very different styles. Not long ago I had a chance to work with two individuals who nicely exemplified the difference between confronting and smoothing over issues.

Head-On Collisions

The first experience involved a leader who loved confrontation and used it quite effectively in her consulting practice. I'll call her Pat Burch. Pat was helping an organization formulate a new strategic position that involved some very sticky issues. The client organization was a hospital group facing a competitive attack from three rivals in one geographic area. Some critical issues arose around positioning the firm vis-à-vis its new competitors. At the beginning of the consulting project, Pat made it very clear to the client that she would not hold anything back, would "tell it like it is," and would fully expect the client to prepare itself for the worst, as well as the best.

As we struggled through a number of strategic issues that had been plaguing the organization for a long time, Pat grew unrelenting in her confrontive style. She would not hesitate taking the client to task on why certain decisions had been made or why issues had not been addressed previously. Every time she heard excuses for why the company had taken this or that position, she confronted the excuse makers and grilled them mercilessly. "How else," she asked, "can I toughen up decision making around here?" As a result of her style, many knock-down, drag-out management sessions took place with the senior executive group. Later, many executives commented that those meetings were among the most brutal and difficult of their careers. Within client organizations, the rumor circulated that Pat would roast you on the spot if you couldn't give solid reasons for your opinions or back up your analysis with facts and dates. As her reputation for probing, questioning, and almost badgering people grew larger, prospective clients, intimidated by the thought of having her drag out all their dirty linen, made sure they had lined up their ducks before asking her to review an issue or evaluate a situation. Nevertheless, when this particular project concluded, I'll never forget how the CEO of the organization praised

Pat for helping the company confront issues it had never fully addressed before: "Her confrontive, open, and candid approach has forced us to break new ground in formulating a strategic position and direction that will benefit us enormously in the years to come."

Steering Clear of Conflict

As a follow-up to the strategy formulation project, the client wanted additional help with implementation. When Pat began the new engagement, she predictably went after every obstacle like a turbocharged bulldozer. This time, however, the client's management team rebelled.

In a long conference with the CEO, Pat herself concluded that while her style had worked wonders in the strategy formulation stage, it would not work now. Clearly unable to handle any more intense confrontation, the company's senior management needed time to heal the wounds that had been inflicted earlier. In the end, the CEO decided to bring in an organizational development specialist with an orientation toward resolving issues more gently.

This new consultant, Paul Kendall, would become the project manager, taking the client through strategy implementation. I observed with pleasure how Paul worked with the senior management team. Instead of aggressively confronting all the problems, issues, and obstacles facing the implementation of the new strategy, he gently and carefully helped people weigh everything within the context of current operations. Members of the management team, not feeling intimidated or threatened, came to grips with implementation issues, such as renovating one wing of the hospital to make it a women's care unit, revitalizing the hospital's emergency center, and developing closer relationships with several outpatient clinics in the area. The team made slow but sure progress with them all. Paul's style did a lot to help the organization recover from the self-inflicted punishment it had suffered while struggling with tough issues during the previous project. His approach was well suited to the implementation issues the company had to address.

Paul taught the management group how to give and receive feedback in positive and gentle ways. He himself always seemed to handle even the thorniest matters without getting into a heated debate or a confrontive standoff. Whenever a confrontation seemed imminent, he would immediately back off in order to avoid the conflict. Then he would cautiously pursue another angle that might get results without undue emotion. The CEO praised the strategy implementation project just as eloquently as he had the prior project. The company did, in fact, go on to implement the new strategy successfully, gaining a stronger competitive position and improved financial performance as well.

To Confront or Not to Confront?

In this case, this is *not* the question. Rather, it's a question of timing. When should you smooth and when should you confront? As in the projects I just cited, confrontation and smoothing both came into play, with the latter most effectively ameliorating the side effects of the former. In the case of my two former colleagues with such markedly different styles, the confronter never became a smoother and the smoother never became a confronter. However, after their experience with this one client, each gained a much greater appreciation for the other's talent. Prior to this engagement, neither of them would have admitted that any style other than his or her own could get the job done. Regardless of your own style, try to keep in mind these two crucial variables: timing and appreciation.

38

Taking Charge
plus
Letting Go

Managers Take Charge; Leaders Let Go

Managers are always trying to *take charge* of people and situations, because they believe that's what the organization expects of them. From meetings and discussions to tasks and assignments, managers assume responsibility for setting agendas, guiding the course of events and measuring performance. The manager's mind says, "If you don't take charge, you're not doing your job."

Leaders take charge, too, but in a different way. No matter how much responsibility a leader may assume over people and situations, he or she would rather *let go*, letting other people take responsibility. Managers know how to let go, too. If they didn't, organizational structures with hierarchies and levels of management would not work. However, managers let go reluctantly, usually wishing they still possessed some degree of control over the details. The leader's soul, on the other hand, says, "If you don't let go, no one else will be sufficiently empowered to make things happen."

A good example of this distinction came up during a consulting engagement I conducted with a midsized professional services firm that provided financial planning, insurance, and legal services through a network of offices. The president, I'll refer to him as Reynolds, had hired a vice president of operations, I'll call him McGrath, to oversee the company's multiple office locations. Reynolds knew how to let go, McGrath loved to take charge. On the surface, the two seemed to complement each other's strengths quite nicely in a classic manager/leader balance that could provide maximum benefits to the organization. Unfortunately, a closer look revealed this not to be the case.

Letting Go Too Soon

Reynolds, wanting to spend more time working on the future of the company, had recognized the need for someone to handle the day-to-day operating concerns raised by different office managers. McGrath would, he hoped, bring a necessary emphasis to operations that would allow the president to focus on acquisitions and long-range planning. Reynolds really did want to let go and delegate the responsibility for day-to-day operations to someone else. McGrath was a take-charge kind of guy who seemed perfectly suited for the job in the beginning. However, as time went on, Reynolds began to get dissatisfied with McGrath's decisions and actions.

Over the years, Reynolds had spent a lot of time inculcating certain operating principles in each of the office managers. These included initiative, accountability, creativity, and empowering others. But now McGrath seemed determined to make decisions and take actions that ran counter to these principles. After this conflict had escalated for several months, Reynolds, although giving McGrath ample time to find a position with another company, finally asked him to resign. Within the company, the rumor mill cranked up and eventually spewed out the theory that Reynolds simply couldn't let go. That's why he fired McGrath. To set the record straight, Reynolds called all the office managers together and communicated to them that far from being unable to let go, he had let go too soon. He went on to explain that although he had honestly wanted to let go of day-to-day operations and delegate them to someone else, he had made the mistake of hiring an individual who did not recognize and accept the operating principles of the organization himself. "Letting go only works if the person who takes charge is sufficiently committed to the principles, values, and purposes of the organization," he concluded. "McGrath was not."

Taking Charge Too Soon

McGrath had been so anxious to take charge that he had moved much too quickly, totally ignoring the organization's strong operating philosophy. Strongly oriented toward taking charge, he had done so with gusto, but unfortunately, he did so with too little attention to the basic principles that guided the organization. Instead, he began immediately making decisions and taking action. It didn't take long for a conflict to arise, because the office managers, deeply committed to the company's operating philosophy, identified very quickly that McGrath was marching out of step. Consequently, the office managers had complained to Reynolds, who himself had begun to conclude that he had let go too soon. In the termination interview between Reynolds and McGrath, the latter did acknowledge that he had been so anxious to demonstrate his competence that he had taken charge of the situation without really analyzing it carefully enough.

Taking Charge and Letting Go in Moderation

The leader may let go too soon, before those who are taking charge can properly carry on the priorities, principles, and purposes of the organization. The manager, on the other hand, may take charge too soon or take charge for too long. In the case just cited, overanxiousness and extremism hurt both the leader and the manager. A little less eagerness on both sides—more care by Reynolds to help McGrath understand and appreciate the company's operating principles and more care by McGrath to learn himself—would have benefited everyone, especially the office managers, who wasted several months in frustration and confusion.

The key when it comes to taking charge and letting go is moderation. Both are vital to any organization, but only in a balanced and integrated organization does moderation mesh them properly. One extreme or the other, unduly shifting between them, or battling over which is best doesn't work as well as a temperate, moderate blending of the take-charge and let-go attitudes.

39

Formality plus Informality

Managers Like Formality; Leaders Prefer Informality

Managers and leaders often differ in their personal preferences as much as they do in their business practices. Managers like orderliness and thus prefer a higher degree of *formality* when it comes to structuring things, interacting with people, presenting ideas, or making decisions. Their minds link successful business operations with formal systems, processes, and procedures. On the other hand, leaders see little or no correlation between formality and success. Leaders also like a certain amount of orderliness, but they don't see why you can't get it in an *informal* way.

A great example of these preferences occurred during the transition from one division president to another in a metal products company a few years ago. The parent company had hired me to take a look at this division and help smooth the organization's adaptation to the new division president's style.

The Formal Past

The parent organization had acquired this division some three years earlier, and now that the existing division president, a quite formal fellow I'll call Conrad, was retiring, top management wanted to install someone more attuned to the parent's informal style. It came as no surprise that Conrad had created a highly formal organization, since he had spent twenty years in the military before becoming president of the company and then division president after it was acquired. Everything that happened in this company went "by the book." There was a form for everything, a policy and procedure behind every form, and an almost military aura behind all policies and procedures. Conrad took great pride in all this, arguing that the organization would continue to run smoothly even if he got hit by a truck.

Ms. Informality Meets Mr. Formality

The new division president, a young woman half her predecessor's age whom I'll call Liz, behaved about as differently from the retiring formal manager as anyone possibly could. Rather informal in her approach, despite an MBA from Stanford, Liz accepted the challenge of repositioning the division for the future. The CEO of the parent company had concluded that Liz's division, which had not met growth projections for two years running, needed a major internal shakeup. Liz took over with great enthusiasm, but found herself wanting to quit after only a week. Whenever she tried to talk informally with people, she found their responses stiff and, as she put it, "all garbled up in formalities." In a private discussion she confided to me that she couldn't get anyone to give her a straight answer. "This company really could run without the 'Old Man' around, and that's what's happening now. It's like Conrad's running the show." As Liz continued trying to make changes, she found herself getting caught up in a tangle of red tape and feeling increasingly frustrated because she couldn't find a way to loosen up the old policies and procedures.

It soon became apparent to me that the people in the organization were unconsciously sabotaging the informality of the new leader. Whenever she wanted to talk issues, strategies, programs, policies, or performance, people reacted as if she had committed some sort of blasphemy against the past. On one occasion, she tried to get a group of employees to evaluate the effectiveness of a policy in the accounting department that specified how to prepare monthly financial statements. Unfortunately, all they did was defend the policy, which was, as you might guess, very formal and traditional. Liz wanted them to consider some new and less formal, more flexible ways for preparing monthly financials that would make them more useful for decision making, but all she got for her trouble was grumbling and foot dragging. One comment that really stung her was, "What you're talking about does not conform to GAAP [generally accepted accounting principles] and it will ruin our financial controls."

The True Source of Order

Before Liz pulled her hair out, I suggested a possible approach that would avoid making the people in the division feel as if they were violating every rule they had spent so much time building and following over the years. I also felt that Liz was overreacting and needed a chance to see the benefits of the company's formal systems and processes. "Identify where the company's formality is positive and where it's not, and then prepare a presentation for discussion with your managers."

In the following months, Liz did so, and to her surprise, she found more positive aspects of the company's formality than she expected. Not surprisingly, she also found a lot of negative effects. One of the negatives lay in the area of financial accounting and reporting, which relied on a slightly outdated IBM shop with not a single microcomputer in sight. This environment made it hard for product and operating managers in the division to use the financial reports for decision making because they needed more flexibility in tying precise cost and revenue data to product lines and market segments than the current system could deliver. As a result, they were keeping their own cobbled-together estimates and records and were often making poor decisions because of them.

To resolve this problem, Liz asked the accounting department to continue its very formal reporting system, but to add to the monthly process a set of reports that utilized the same database but could be adapted and modified as needed by division managers. She ordered personal computers and Lotus 1-2-3 for key people not as a substitute for the formal system, but as a complement. Over time, the accounting department did become more informal and flexible in its approach to management information, but without abandoning the formality of the standard financial accounting and reporting system. To her credit, Liz came to the conclusion that formality in some vital areas actually worked better than informality. By the same token, the introduction of informality in some areas reduced a lot of unnecessary red tape and unproductive bureaucracy. The combination of formality and informality gradually began to work its way throughout the division as the positive experience in the accounting department was told and retold. The division went on to hit its growth targets, and Liz gained a deeper understanding of the benefits of both formal and informal approaches.

Both formality and informality can be extremely beneficial if applied properly within an organization. Unfortunately, most people and organizations favor one or the other and rarely seem to be able to achieve a nonadversarial and effective blend. Here managers and leaders can work side by side for the best results and for a truly empowered environment by carefully assessing the pros and cons of formal and informal approaches and then aligning them with those areas where they can do the most good.

40

Science plus Art

Managers Venerate Science; Leaders Revere Art

Managers think of their work as a precise, rational, and quantitative *science*. Leaders, valuing the fluid, intuitive, and qualitative side of their work, think of it more as an *art*. Given these tendencies, managers study, define, and try to clarify the concrete, measurable aspects of organizations and management, while leaders try to capture feelings, dreams, hopes, and beliefs. Most of today's executives are part scientist and part artist, although most lean in one direction or the other. Without both, however, you cannot create the ultimate capitalistic engine.

I have been fortunate enough to experience first hand how one chief executive officer, Philip Brandon (not his real name), seems to perfectly blend the science and art of management and leadership. Having consulted over the years for his company, I became quite close to Philip and spent a good deal of personal time with him. Naturally, we talked a lot about his business, and I soon learned the story of his rise to the top of a very large organization.

Removing the Tension Between Science and Art

We had both graduated from the Harvard Business School, although Philip had received his degree ten years earlier than I. Like many contemporary executives professionally trained at a business school, Philip's career had begun with a heavy emphasis on the science of management. Early on he felt a deep disdain for people in the company who claimed to rely on gut feeling and intuitive decision making. Thus he tried to resolve the natural tension between science and art by removing the art. Basically, he ignored the artistic side, affording it no place in anyone's repertoire of skills. He took this approach for over ten years, during which his innate brilliance and high energy level propelled him quickly up the organization and gained for him a reputation as a tough-as-nails professional executive. A vice president after ten years, Philip gradually began to mellow, recognizing that his scientific view of the world was not necessarily the only one. He had discovered through experience that intuitive decision making, qualitative considerations, and "soft" skills did, in fact, have a place in an organization's repertoire of capabilities. Slowly he began to value, at least partially, the skills of leadership.

Fighting the Tension Between Science and Art

During the next ten years, which took him to the position of chief operating officer of a company that now boasted several billion dollars a year in revenue, Philip found himself placing less rigidly quantitative executives in creative areas such as product development and marketing, while choosing more scientific ones for positions in manufacturing and finance. Still, although he had come to recognize some of the value of intuitive artful decision making and management, Philip would not award it equal weight with the professional, rational, and scientific approach to management in which he had been initially trained. As he worked with the men and women in his organization, he constantly struggled with and fought the tension between science and art. Later, as he reflected on this period of his career, Philip admitted that his bias toward the scientific side of management usually dominated his every move. Yet, as his appreciation of the art of management grew, so did his awareness of the tension between the two. He felt as though he were a tennis ball, bouncing back and forth between science and art in an attempt to resolve this tension, which did nothing but increase.

After twenty years, coincidental with his rise to chairman and CEO of the company, Philip finally concluded that he had been wrong to fight the tension between the science and art of management. Now, over the last five years, he has been trying a new approach.

Tapping the Tension Between Science and Art

All Philip really did was redefine the equation, changing his perception of the tension from a problem to an untapped resource. The natural tension between science and art, he discovered, actually made the process of management and leadership much more effective, beneficial, and productive. When he simply allowed the tension to exist with no attempts to remove or fight it, both managers and leaders seemed to benefit. In this kind of management/leadership environment, managers and leaders weren't battling each other, positioning themselves against each other, selling each other, or debating each other. Instead, they came to enjoy and appreciate each other's differences. To create this kind of environment, Philip began consciously fostering and discussing this natural tension as an important resource with his key people. In this way, the tension brought a tempering influence to bear on both managers and leaders, helping each improve his or her own individual management style and increase appreciation for others. Philip described his new motto as "appreciate the tension." This motto has a rich depth behind it, because it suggests that managers and leaders should appreciate not only their different orientations, but also how those orientations naturally clash and can be used to strengthen each other and the whole organization. In the long run, this long-time friend and superb executive did not allow the tension to become a conflict, contention, or point of serious disagreement, but rather he used it to increase awareness and understanding.

For example, I watched Philip in a meeting with two of his very aggressive senior executives, one more of a leader, the other more of a manager. As they discussed the wisdom of a proposed entry into a new market, there appeared to be a growing conflict that, left unresolved, might create an unnecessary schism within the company. Philip brilliantly nudged each of the executives to continue discussing their points of view respectively. One executive favored an aggressive and dramatic entry into the new market that would require substantial resources and commitment from the company. The other executive favored a slower, more cautious market entrance that would build to a crescendo over several years. There were merits to both positions. Philip never allowed the tension to become too much of a conflict, yet he permitted it to increase to a level that allowed each of the executives to more totally grasp the other's perspective.

At this particular point in the discussion, Philip reminded his two executives that they had risen to their respective posts because they had remained true to their orientations. This, they should continue to do, but now, as they prepared for even greater responsibilities in their professional careers, they needed to also transcend their inherent perspectives to appreciate other viewpoints more readily. The tension began turning into tempered understanding as the two executives began discussing in a give-and-take manner how to best go about entering the new market. Later, one of the executives commented that he had learned more in that one afternoon about management and leadership than he had in his entire career. Specifically, he said he realized as never before that true management and leadership meant drawing out the best from opposing forces in order to blend them together for extraordinary results.

41

Duties plus Dreams

Managers Perform Duties, Leaders Pursue Dreams

In their drive to become effective, managers focus on *duties* because duties represent concrete and finite tasks. When managers introspectively evaluate their performance, strengths, and weaknesses, they instinctively use current duties, professional and personal, as their standards of measurement. When leaders want to enhance their effectiveness, they pursue *dreams* because dreams represent future and infinite possibilities. As leaders conduct self-evaluations to assess how well they are doing, dreams, not duties, provide the standards of measurement.

The ways in which duties and dreams function in an organization came dramatically to light as I consulted with an associate who had recently taken over a company. In every way a leader, this executive dreamed of creating an organization that would allow other people to follow their own dreams. In the beginning, this man's leadership seemed to be paying off brilliantly, as the once-stodgy company shifted emphasis and began creating an environment in which executives and managers could pursue imaginative agendas and build their own businesses within the company.

According to the CEO's dream, the parent company would own not more than 49 percent of its subsidiaries or divisions, thus affording the owners of these business units the appropriate incentive and opportunity to build their empires and fulfill their dreams. The CEO imagined a sort of corporate "incubator" for small and midsized companies, in which they could enjoy some protection provided by the nurturing parent's umbrella while at the same time developing and flourishing into their own independent entities. Despite an auspicious beginning, however, the dream soon began to run up against some rocky realities.

Neglected Duties

As this CEO implemented his dream of creating a corporate environment that would foster the development of others' dreams, he seemed to be laying the ground work for a truly innovative approach to managing business enterprises. He made three initial acquisitions whose previous owners retained majority ownership yet benefited from the financial capability of the parent company, which enabled them to grow much more rapidly than they would have on their own. As these companies came into the corporate family, everyone expressed excitement over the fact that the pursuit of their dreams seemed more tangible and possible than ever. Everything started out well. Then, little by little, the flaw in his concept became apparent: No company could live solely on its dreams. Focusing only on dreams, to the neglect of duties, led to the CEO's failure to establish clear expectations and parameters for people and operations throughout the company. Some of the newly acquired company executives, as well as executives from existing operations, began complaining that they received no guidance, direction, or help from the CEO. These complaints turned into criticism as the CEO pursued his own dreams to expand internationally and give birth to yet other dreams. As he did so, he was becoming less and less accessible, setting an example of disregard for mundane duties that began to affect the entire organization.

Success requires performance of certain duties relating to management systems, financial and marketing analysis, strategic planning, and a whole host of other tasks. In the CEO's world of dreams, these did not seem to really matter much. Instead, the dreams of people overruled all else. Over time, what began as a minor problem grew into a major crisis.

On several occasions I chatted with the CEO regarding the need for more guidance in the organization. Performing duties need not prevent the pursuit of dreams, I argued. In fact, I felt the dream could shatter under the weight of neglected duties. He listened to me, but as it turned out, he never really believed what I said.

Neglected Dreams

Over the next few years, the company ran into difficulty as all the neglected duties began catching up with it. The CEO watched as one of the acquired companies went out of business, another one's management demanded a buy-out, and a third had to be scaled back significantly. The overall company was experiencing only marginal returns, and the future looked even worse unless something happened immediately. Perhaps in panic, the CEO orchestrated a massive shift from dreams to duties. He brought in some outside financial advisors and systems consultants to help establish the corporate guidelines, systems, and processes that had been missing. There was a flurry of activity and a lot of attention to corporate duty, but still something was not right. I distinctly remember how the countenance of the CEO changed during this period of time. It was as if the light had gone out. Now the pendulum had swung the other way, and before long the dreams began suffering from neglect. Duties ruled the day: new management systems were put into place, new directions were charted, and new businesses were targeted with the goal that management ensure the success of these operations with an emphasis on duties.

As I observed this company and attempted to advise its CEO, I realized how the organization had changed from a cloud of great dreams to a cave of great duties. The once-vibrant spirit within the company had disappeared. Eventually the CEO presided over the final paring down, then liquidation of the company's assets, except for a minor ownership position in a large service firm that required little or no hands-on management. The CEO basically closed down the operations of this company, turned over the remaining relatively passive portion to the board of directors, and left to follow a new dream.

Dreams Require Duties

It takes vibrant dreams to create a vibrant company. My friend had placed such an inordinate emphasis on dreams, however, that he forgot that the conversion of dreams into realities requires the performance of certain duties. He led, but he couldn't manage and he failed to effectively enlist the help of those who could. As much as he tried to perform his corporate duties and reverse the neglect that had occurred, his heart and soul were never really in it. In the end, he found himself unwilling and unable to combine dreams and duties.

In the case of dreams and duties, few organizations can thrive on just one or the other. I could argue that dreams are most important and should precede duties, or I could argue that duties are most vital because they make dreams possible. In reality, I believe these two are inexorably linked, and too little or too much focus on one or the other in an organization will cause suboptimal performance or failure.

VI

Bottom-Line Performance/ Results

Performance and results have always been the hallmark of successful organizations and people. The future will be no different, even though our understanding of what leads to superior performance may be greatly heightened and our definition of results may be ever broader, more comprehensive, and balanced. One-dimensional orientations toward only the tangible short-term results (manifested by management-dominated organizations) or toward only intangible long-term results (evidenced by leadership-driven organizations) will not work as well in the future as they may have in the past. Sometimes these narrow perspectives will make sense in particular circumstances, but for organizations that want to sustain superior performance in the future, both management and leadership must come into play in just the right doses at just the right time. Conflict-oriented organizations will fail to achieve optimal status because the adversarial relationship created within them will make true integration impossible. Of course, vacillation-prone organizations will not know which side is up and will seldom attain anything but marginal or negative results.

Balanced and integrated organizations will define performance and results in the broadest ways possible, taking into account all stakeholders and the full impact of the organization on the lives of people that work in or are otherwise affected by the organization. Such organizations will value all orientations and perspectives.

In this section you will see how managers and leaders differ in their orientations toward bottom-line performance and results, and you'll see some ways in which you can exploit these fundamental differences to reach peak levels of performance in the future.

42

Performance plus Potential

Managers Scrutinize Performance; Leaders Search for Potential

When it comes to looking at people's abilities and accomplishments, managers prefer to rely on *performance* appraisals. Past and current performance, managers feel, best reflects the value of a subordinate or employee. Managers only pay minor attention to potential because potential is so much more abstract and uncertain than other more current and quantifiable factors. Of course, this is the very reason potential attracts leaders in their evaluations of people. For leaders, *potential* represents the real power of the future. Given this difference in focus, leaders tend to groom leaders and managers tend to groom managers; leaders looking for potential and managers looking for performance.

So what happens when you have leaders evaluating managers and managers evaluating leaders? I observed the problems this can pose when I helped a large aerospace company evaluate the impact of what it called a "high potential" program designed to identify key managers and leaders throughout the organization who would most likely rise to the top in the next decade. The company wanted to make sure these people received the kinds of experiences they needed to lead and manage the company into the next century.

High Potential

The program had pinpointed 100 high-potential people at the two management levels just below the senior executives. Of these 100, between 25 and 30 would end up filling senior slots in the next decade. The others would remain in division executive or staff executive positions. As I expected, of the 100 total high-potential people, some were leaders and some were managers. And, as I also expected, the leader-type high potentials had generally been identified by senior leaders; the manager-type high potentials, by senior managers. I saw one important difference between those identified by leaders and those identified by managers. The ones identified by leaders possessed certain but sometimes almost indefinable characteristics and attitudes, while those identified by managers displayed concrete past and current high performance. In some cases, high-potential leaders had demonstrated little or no high performance in the past or present. Obviously, the leaders who identified those people as high potentials were seeing and sensing something that couldn't be measured by current or past performance.

In order to distinguish between the leader-identified high-potential people and the manager-identified high-potential people (in a few cases it was difficult to impossible), I designated the leader-identified group as "high potentials" and manager-identified group as "high performers."

To broaden the high potentials' and high performers' experience and prepare them for general management responsibilities, the company moved many of them around the company, so that they could learn more about both staff and line responsibilities in operations, marketing, finance, and so on. When a high potential reported to a leader, this worked just fine, but when he or she reported to a manager, problems quickly arose. In every case I observed, the manager-type senior executive ran into a great deal of difficulty trying to evaluate the leader-type high potential. Attempting to focus solely on performance as the criterion for evaluation, the manager usually looked for hard evidence, ignoring the potential that had moved a particular high potential into his or her present position. Oftentimes managers were totally baffled as to why a high-potential person had been labeled such, indicating a major difference in the very basis of judgment between managers and leaders.

My observations led me to conclude, preliminarily, that managers are very poor at evaluating leaders. Never fully appreciating the leader's capabilities, managers find it hard to capture, quantify, and evaluate the work of leaders. Trying to fit a leader into a manager's framework of performance appraisal is like trying to fit a square peg in a round hole.

High Performance

The flip side of this problem, which turned out to be just as significant for this company, occurred when leaders tried to evaluate high performers. Leader-type senior executives had trouble evaluating high performers reporting to them because they looked for potential but could only see performance track records.

Because the high performers did not demonstrate the kind of leadership traits and attitudes that the leader-type senior executives were looking for, the latter could not fully value the track record of performance that had propelled a particular high performer up in the organization. Of course, the leader-type senior executives valued the record of performance, but when they failed to see leadership traits, such as vision and the ability to empower others, they wondered whether these high performers could really guide the company through the next twenty years. In both cases, the manager/leader or leader/manager relationship tended to be plagued with communication problems, which further complicated an evaluation of performance or potential.

Too Little Time for Evaluation, Training, and Development

During the course of my study, I became even more sensitive to the manager/leader dichotomy and began studying examples of it more closely. In the end, I concluded that this organization simply did not spend enough time evaluating, communicating with, trying to understand, training, and developing its midlevel executives. Ironically, the business press invariably refers to this company as a very well run one that prides itself on spending a great deal of time on executive development and issues of management succession. How much more excellent might it become, I wondered, if its senior executives made better decisions because they spent more time understanding and developing the manager/leader mix? Too many people were being promoted improperly, and others, passed over for the wrong reasons, were leaving the company for better jobs elsewhere. Hence I proposed to my client that if senior executives spent more time evaluating high potentials and high performers, they would automatically further develop, broaden, and deepen their own understanding about the management and leadership needs of the company now and in the future. Typically, when a manager-type senior executive linked up with a leader-type midlevel executive, or vice versa, each would pass off shortcomings in communication, evaluation, and training as simply a difference in style. Unfortunately, this happened again and again and again in the company, until far too many midlevel executives were untrained, underdeveloped, and inappropriately evaluated.

I also suggested that the evaluation process combine both performance and potential factors, which would make it more of a learning experience for both the evaluator and the person being evaluated. If managers could better understand the importance of potential, they would broaden their perspectives and become more effective groomers of talent. By the same token, if leaders could better understand the importance of performance, they would become expanded and more comprehensive in the ways they helped people up the corporate ladder.

In the beginning, all this seemed too philosophical to my client, and the senior executives displayed a certain amount of resistance to my recommendations. However, a few months later, they did change their evaluation process in an effort to weigh more equally the importance of a person's track record of performance and his or her potential to negotiate the challenges of the future. Once the company had gained a good deal of experience over several months with its new approach to evaluation, it began improving its batting average with promotions by a measurable margin. I might also add that the senior executives in this company gained a new appreciation for the blending of management and leadership.

43

Dependence plus Independence

Managers Are Dependent; Leaders Are Independent

Managers depend on established organizations to do their jobs. Like the engine in a Formula 1 racing car, the manager functions best within a well-defined and supportive structure. Managers, after all, would not even exist without such structures. As a result of their relationship to systems, processes, and programs, managers tend to be somewhat *dependent* people, but in the best sense of the word. They depend on the organization; the organization depends on them. Take a manager out of an organization, and both suffer, the manager feeling lonely, powerless, and frustrated and the organization drifting off the track.

Leaders, on the other hand, function *independently* of established organizations, even when they are an integral part of them. Like a designer of sports cars, leaders exhilarate in a sense of independence, regardless of any necessary support systems. Even without structures, systems, processes, and programs, leaders can still thrive. They may participate in such structures and programs or even create them, but they do not derive their identities from them.

As a result, most leaders have a hard time appreciating the sort of positive dependence managers relish. And for their part, most managers feel uncomfortable with the freewheeling independence leaders crave. This often makes working together to achieve performance and results very difficult, as I recently saw in a rapidly growing winter sports equipment manufacturing and marketing company. This $30 million company asked me to take a close look at its organizational structure with the hope that I might be able to help it alter the structure to overcome rampant communications problems and thus improve performance.

Too Much Dependence Can Stunt a Person's Growth

I began my investigation with a series of indepth interviews of senior managers. By the time I finished the first round of interviews, I had heard the same story of "management misfires" at least five times. As the story went, the company had hired a "supermanager" from a large consumer products company two years ago. This fellow came aboard as the vice president of marketing, with a clear mandate to upgrade the company's marketing systems, processes, and structure. Not long after the supermanager arrived, he began complaining about the lack of certain data, or the faultiness of this system, or the folly of that methodology, procedure, or policy. To most people in the organization, this manager quickly became a nuisance.

After about six months, the company president began to feel pressure from the other vice presidents and even lower-level marketing and sales managers to get the new marketing vice president to "put up or shut up." By this people meant that the supermanager should spend a lot more time correcting problems and a lot less time complaining about them. After ten months on the job, problems in the supermanager's area had, in fact, done nothing but get worse. Not surprisingly, he left the company before his first anniversary. According to the storytellers I interviewed, the lack of established information and reporting systems, sales and marketing programs, and any really formal structure at all had completely immobilized the fellow. At his previous job he had grown so dependent on a well-oiled system and formal structure that he couldn't function without them. Nor could he create them himself, because he couldn't exercise the independence needed to do so.

Too Much Independence Can Drive a Person Nuts

As the saga unfolded, the president, feeling burned by having hired the supermanager, went completely in the opposite direction and next hired a "superleader" to whip the marketing function into shape. The superleader waded in like a wild man, jumping from system to system and idea to idea as he constantly experimented with new ways of doing things. According to the storytellers, the company embarked on and aborted at least a dozen different approaches until the superleader also left the company without even having learned the names of most of the people in his department. Clearly, he had gotten so caught up in his own whirlwind of agendas that he never connected with the rest of the organization. As a result, the communications situation had grown to crisis levels by the time I arrived on the scene. Now the company desperately wanted to avoid striking out a third time.

Dependence plus Independence Equals Interdependence

After the initial interviews and some preliminary analysis, I gave the president of the company a preliminary status report that suggested upgrading the company's marketing function by bringing around the qualities of each of the last two marketing vice presidents. Unfortunately, I went on, such perfect combinations rarely reside in a single individual. Therefore, I suggested an organizational structure that would promote more interaction and interdependence. Since my initial interviews indicated widespread awareness of the problems facing the company, and since my early analysis indicated that functional areas had become too isolated and separated from one another, I proposed an organizational approach that would help dependent managers and independent leaders benefit from each other's orientations. Such a blending would, perhaps, eliminate extreme dependent or independent behavior.

What does such an interdependent organization look like? Pretty much like any other from the outside. However, the people in it function differently because they become neither overly dependent nor independent. Rather, they value both the dependent and independent modes and therefore take advantage of both. People in interdependent organizations are dependent on some systems or processes, but never become so dependent that they don't still operate independently of them from time to time. In fact, it is this independent orientation that serves to improve systems and processes. In this way, both dependent and independent orientations become intertwined and interdependent, creating a management/ leadership environment with more openness, discussion, give and take, and true progress.

The president bought my recommendations and soon promoted one of his younger marketing managers, a leader by orientation, to marketing vice president. He also pulled a more dependent person into the number two position in the marketing department. The new interdependent approach would encourage the two to interact frequently. Still, I urged the president to closely monitor the dependence/independence balance to ensure the desired level of interdependence. In the end, he began building what he really wanted: a company that fostered interdependence rather than excessive dependence or independence.

44

Compensation plus Satisfaction

Managers Compensate People; Leaders Satisfy Them

Managers tend to focus on providing for their people's material needs by awarding them proper *compensation*, paying them fair wages for work well done. By doing so, they strike a sort of bargain with their people: "For X amount of work, we will pay you Y number of dollars." Logical. Straightforward. Operationally practical. Leaders, on the other hand, prefer to focus on the *satisfaction* of more than mere material needs, viewing compensation as an important, but minor part of overall satisfaction. Leaders strike a different sort of bargain with their people: "For X amount of work, we will supply Y amount of satisfaction in terms of dollars, work environment, opportunity, challenge, growth, and sense of fulfillment." Authentic. Complete. Forward-looking.

Recently, while conducting interviews at an industrial products manufacturing firm preliminary to a series of management retreats, I was struck by the degree to which employees were preoccupied with the company's new incentive compensation system.

The system was quite a creative one, with promotions tied to performance goals and bonuses and raises depending on overall corporate productivity and profitability.

Interestingly, the people I interviewed expressed dramatically different attitudes toward the program, with some raving about its positive value and others feeling it really missed the point and did not stimulate greater productivity. Talks with two employees in particular uncovered the extremes.

Compensating but Not Satisfying

The manager who most admired the new incentive compensation system, I'll call him Ted, pointed out that by adjusting it to match the needs of different employees, he could directly tackle the problems of lack of focus and low productivity among certain of his people. Such problems, he argued, resulted from the confusion employees felt about their jobs and the expectations of management. The new incentive compensation system could help reduce such confusion by sharpening peoples' awareness of priorities and expectations. When I asked about other, less tangible job satisfaction factors, Ted agreed, in principle at least, that they were important. However, he still felt strongly that money, far from being the root of all evil, was the root of all productivity. His views interested me because, clearly, his soul told him that it takes more than money to motivate people to peak levels of performance, but his mind still placed a premium on cold, hard cash.

As I turned the interview toward other pressing issues facing the company, I discovered that a very basic belief ruled Ted's thinking about his own job: People work, first and foremost, for a paycheck. If used properly, he believed, that paycheck could powerfully direct and reinforce an employee's actions. At one point he even said, "All this corporate culture and high-commitment work environment stuff is great, but the bottom line is what a person takes to the bank."

Satisfying but Not Compensating

In sharp contrast to the preceding was a budding leader at the other extreme, I'll call her Anne, the one who believed that the new compensation system missed the point. Productivity and focus, she insisted, were derived not from dollars, but from satisfying a person's deepest desires and needs. Acceptance, recognition, belonging, and self-actualization motivate people far more than cash incentives ever will. She put it nicely: "Compensation, incentive-based or otherwise, is just lunch money." Anne compared an organization to a basketball team, where pride and team spirit, more than the salaries of individual stars, create winning seasons and bring championship banners to the home arena. She said, "We have to figure out what *really* satisfies each of our people, and then help them get what they want within the context of company objectives. If we try but fail, then maybe we've got the wrong employee and both of us would be better off if we went our separate ways." Anne did not dismiss the need for fair compensation, because money, she felt, does help people fulfill their basic material needs, but she also believed that it could never serve as a source of deeper satisfaction. It's the deeper satisfaction that drives people to excel. As I probed deeper into her fundamental values, I found that she believed that highly satisfied people would forego significant increases in compensation if it meant losing or lowering satisfaction. "We worry too much about the almighty dollar in this company," she concluded.

Compensating and Satisfying Together

About a year later I visited this company again to see how the new compensation system had worked out. After spending some time with the two people I had interviewed earlier, I was not much surprised by their experiences. Ted said he had seen mixed results. "My weakest people did show some strong improvement," he said. "But my best people turned in about the same results. A few even slipped. Overall, I'd say it was a wash." Anne confided much the same. "By and large, we made a little progress, but next year's going to be a bear cat because I lost three of my top performers to the competition."

No incentive compensation system provides all the cures for what ails a company. In reality, both compensation and satisfaction play crucial roles in organizational and individual achievement. One without the other will never give you the results you can get by harnessing them together in a balanced way.

Ted was a true manager with little real appreciation for human satisfiers other than the financial kind. Anne was a true leader who appreciated the power you can generate with people who obtain high degrees of deeper satisfaction. Overemphasis on the former perspective leads to an overly practical, mundane, and materialistic approach, while too much stress on the latter can become too intangible to grasp.

45

Conserving plus Risking

Managers Conserve Assets; Leaders Risk Them

The mind of the manager is *conservative* in more ways than one. It almost always adopts a protective viewpoint when it comes to assets. Of course, that viewpoint demotes risk to a secondary consideration. Paradoxically, the manager does eagerly risk assets, but only when doing so will conserve them. The manager's motto is, "The less risk, the more sure the reward."

In contrast, the soul of the leader tends toward *risking* assets in order to achieve and obtain more of them. It insists that the best way to conserve assets is to risk them constantly. For leaders, conservation of assets remains a secondary consideration. According to leaders, since a firm's assets always lie in jeopardy, risk comes constantly into play. The leader says, "The more risk, the greater the reward."

This contrast became acutely apparent to me during my involvement with the husband and wife cofounders of a large architectural design firm who ran the operation as a team. As I soon found out, each of them brought a uniquely valuable orientation to the organization. The firm maintained six offices across the country and one international office in Brazil. Together these generated annual revenues of $300 million from design fees, construction contracts, and interior installations. On average, the company obtained a 28 percent return on assets.

Risking It All

The wife, Leigh (not her real name), was a leader, constantly searching out opportunities to build and expand the business. Driven by an overwhelming desire for success and with absolutely no fear of failure, she stood willing to bet the company's entire future any day of the week. So what if she failed? She could always build it up again because she was such a superb marketer and never, even in times of difficulty, lost the admiration of all her employees and clients.

However, the company did not always bet on her ambitious ideas and plans. For example, when she was tempted to buy a large Houston-based construction firm with twice the revenue volume of her own company, her husband, Joel (not his real name), finally convinced her to back off because the target area's economic downturn seemed to spell certain problems.

Eventually, Leigh found a gamble that seemed a bit less risky. Still, she ended up leveraging the company's assets, as well as her and her husband's personal fortune, behind an extremely risky high-rise office space development that would have put her company out of business if it didn't succeed. This risk not only inspired her, she used it to rouse employees to throw their hearts and souls into the project. Well, the high-rise development project worked brilliantly, catapulting the company well ahead of its competitors in the area. But it wasn't just because Leigh wanted to risk it all.

Conserving It All

At least half the credit for the project's success went to Joel, a committed manager. A shrewd, skeptical businessman, Joel could not motivate or inspire people the way Leigh did. But he did know how to conserve his assets. Over the years, his prudence balanced his wife's brilliant, but risky, ideas, such as the proposed purchase of the Houston-based construction firm. But Joel had agreed to risk the company's and his own personal assets on the high-rise office space development project because without such a bold move, the company could have lost its carefully cultivated position in the primary metropolitan market. The risk, as he saw it, was a necessary step to conserve assets, much of which related to market position, reputation, and visibility.

In these two cases at least, the conservation viewpoint helped separate the unnecessary risks from the necessary ones, and although an ongoing and fundamental difference of opinion ignited many heated discussions between the partners, in the end both got what they wanted from the enterprise.

Calculated Risks

A deep and genuine respect between the cofounders formed the very root of the design firm's success. Not only did Leigh and Joel enjoy a strong and loving marriage, they truly respected and valued each other's opposing orientations and differing talents. As a result, they prospered in a volatile industry where many competitors have stagnated or gone "belly up" because of too much risk or too much conservation.

Executives in other industries can profit from this example, especially if they can see that a successful strategy often involves a marriage of prudence and boldness. A lot of business consultants talk about taking "calculated risks," but they usually recommend either a conservation strategy or a risk strategy rather than conservation combined with risk. This is an important distinction. Too many managers and leaders fall victim to an "either-or" mentality that inevitably deteriorates into an adversarial relationship between the prudent and the bold. It's better, I think, to adopt a "combined with" mentality that recognizes that we're all in this together. This is where the balanced and integrated organization with its empowering management/leadership environment out-shines the other types of organizations. Only the balanced and integrated organization stresses the "combined with" or "blended" orientation capable of properly mixing risk with conservation for a "one plus one equals three" result.

46

Tangible
plus
Intangible

Managers Pursue the Tangible; Leaders Seek the Intangible

The mind of the manager may think both in terms of tangible and intangible results, but it tends to think first and foremost of the *tangible*. The soul of the leader also may acknowledge the need for both tangible and intangible results, but it usually puts *intangible* ahead of tangible. While managers tend to seek, first, tangible and quantitative results, such as profits, sales growth, market share, number of new locations opened, new customers acquired, return on investment, and so forth, leaders tend to pursue, first, intangible and qualitative results, such as the satisfaction level of employees, the strength of customer relationships, the level of confidence displayed by the lending institutions that finance the company's working capital, and so forth. For managers, tangible results clearly define progress toward the objectives of their organizations. Managers prefer tangible results because they are so real, concrete, and graspable. For leaders, however, intangible results reveal more about the quality and essence of their organizations. Thus leaders spend time assessing the intangible results they believe ultimately deliver the tangible results.

Last year I worked with a management consulting firm whose managing partner, a fellow I'll call A. E. Pearson, dealt largely in intangible results. Having set the goals of building a strong organizational competence in key areas within the firm and of nurturing long-term client relationships, he had helped the firm grow to the point where it fielded over 200 professionals in eight offices around the world. However, a couple of partners on the management committee had become more and more concerned about the way Pearson seemed to discount tangible results, which had been weakening over the past two years. Of course, these two partners behaved much more like managers than leaders.

The Chicken-and-the-Egg Syndrome

Just prior to my getting involved with this firm, the debate over tangible versus intangible results had come to a head with Pearson barely on speaking terms with his two unhappy colleagues. After many discussions of why such tangible results as project profitability and return of investment had waned recently, it became clear to all concerned that the company must, first and foremost, resolve the disagreement about how the firm should be run. Pearson argued passionately that the intangibles, such as customer satisfaction and consultant competence, would ultimately deliver top-flight financial performance. He strongly felt that any large shift in focus away from the intangible toward the tangible would cause the firm to lose sight of its identity, its values, and its purpose. For example, Pearson felt that it was by far more important to make sure the client was satisfied than it was to make sure a client project was profitable. Of course, profitability was important to him, but not nearly so important as client satisfaction. If it meant losing money on a project to ensure client satisfaction, Pearson would not hesitate. Of course, he expected to correct a loss on future projects, but he knew there wouldn't be any future projects if the client felt dissatisfied. His opponents argued just as vehemently that only close attention to tangible results would reverse the negative trend. Until the reversal happened, the intangibles weren't worth much. This "which came

first, the chicken or the egg" debate among the management committee became so draining and detrimental to the firm that Pearson
confided to me that he had decided to step down.

Hatching Confusion

The management committee voted to replace Pearson with his
most vocal opponent. Like a conquering hero, the new managing
partner, I'll call him E. A. Dearborn, assumed his responsibilities
with a vengeance, immediately requiring that each of the eight
offices report financial and operating performance on a weekly
basis. Soon Dearborn had imposed rigorous tangible guidelines,
replete with all the concrete measures, ratios, and performance
indicators that would help the firm reverse its waning performance. The new program required each of the eight office managing partners to submit an elaborate monthly report that took days
to complete. Before long, of course, these reports stimulated more
dread than results.

This is when the company hired me to take a look at its turmoil
and help it understand why the recent measures had generated so
much confusion and unrest. As I did, I found that the debate within
the management committee between tangible and intangible results had now filtered throughout the organization, eating up a lot
of valuable time within each of the eight offices. In some cases, the
office managing partner fueled the debate because he or she so
intensely disliked the new reporting requirements and all the time
and energy they wasted. In other cases, the pressure and resentment came from below. In no case had the new approach achieved
the expected turnaround. The management committee wanted to
know why.

After analyzing several months of accumulated tangible measures compiled by each of the offices, and after conducting a number
of interviews with key people, I asked the management committee
to set aside two days for a discussion designed to get to the bottom
of things.

The Egg Really Does Come First

At the beginning of the retreat, I framed an initial proposition that fueled heated discussions over the next two days: "The firm's history indicates that it obtains the best tangible results from an intangible focus." In other words, I proposed that the "egg," namely, the level of competence of professionals within the firm, relationships with clients, the quality of work delivered, and client satisfaction, did indeed come first. The "chicken," that is, quantitative or tangible results, came later. The recent downturn in the firm's financial performance did not come about as a function of an intangible focus, but rather as a function of increased competitiveness in the marketplace and the rapid growth of the firm itself. In view of increased competitiveness and rapid growth, the company needed now, more than ever, to concentrate on the intangibles.

While I stressed that by no means should the firm disregard tangible results, I did urge that it realign its priorities to focus on intangibles first and tangibles as the expected byproduct.

Without going into all the details of what happened during those two days, during which the emotions and thoughts of the management committee flowed from one extreme to another, I can report that the team finally agreed to focus first on intangible results and then on tangible ones. At the end of the second day, the team almost unanimously agreed to reinstate Pearson, while assigning Dearborn to the tracking of specific financial performance indicators. Predictably, the only contrary vote came from Dearborn. Not long after this meeting, Dearborn left the firm by letting his partners buy him out. In his absence, the remaining members of the management committee and the office managing partners began to shift their emphasis back to the old way without neglecting the needed tangible results. In this way, the firm became more aware of the importance of tangibles, while realizing that the long-term success of the firm hinged on intangibles.

Currently, the firm continues to grapple with issues of competitiveness and growth, but it does so with a new unity, letting intangible results drive the tangible results. The firm has become stronger and has made inroads into previously unserved market areas.

Most companies today live with great pressure for financial performance, which consequently often becomes the primary focus. Unfortunately, such companies succumb to these pressures for tangible results by neglecting intangible results, which only exacerbates any performance problem. In my view, the only way to ensure tangible results is to focus on the intangible ones first and then to make sure the tangible results follow. Both are essential to long-term success. But, in this case, you must put the egg before the chicken.

47

Present plus Future

Managers Inhabit the Present; Leaders Reside in the Future

Managers' minds think about and act on the *present*. When managers do peek into the future, they generally do so by extrapolating from the past and present. In any business, managers must project ahead in terms of expansion, financing, marketing, or production considerations, but in their daily jobs they much prefer to reside in the present. They can see, feel, and grasp the present but grow quite anxious thinking too much about the future. For managers, the present represents the parameters of their accountability. They can't do anything about the past, and the only way to create the future is to manage the present.

Leaders' souls, on the other hand, reside in the *future*, viewing the present mostly in terms of its long-range implications. For leaders, the present functions primarily as a measure of progress toward some future envisioned state. The future seems quite real and graspable to leaders. Leaders perceive their accountability to be defined in terms of future change, progress, or results. Leaders eat, drink, and sleep the future while seeing the present as simply the transition point from past to future.

I recently observed the demise of an emerging business that would have become very successful if only its two founding partners could have found a way to communicate their very different perspectives about what the business should be. A promising regional distribution firm, the company dealt in industrial supplies and equipment, a market that offered the potential for enormous growth. However, the impasse between the partners became so great that it ended up literally destroying the company.

A friend of the two founding partners had invited me to come in and look at the company to see if I could help avert disaster. As it turned out, I could do little but watch it unfold.

Stepping from A to B

One of the founding partners, I'll call him Hank, was a manager stuck firmly in the present. Looking into the future made him extremely uncomfortable because he couldn't get a handle on it. "I'm not a fortune teller," he was fond of saying. As a result, he took a plodding one-foot-in-front-of-the-other approach to distributorship. His idea of growth was to move from A to B, B to C, and C to D. Any attempt at point A to get him to consider C, D, E, or beyond made him dig in his heels. For example, if Hank were presented with the opportunity to distribute two new products, he would accept only one of them at a time in order to ensure the proper handling of each. He didn't think about the future effect of losing or postponing distribution of the other product, he only thought in terms of distributing one new product now. After that product was on board, he'd worry about the next one. Since Hank had participated in several other businesses that had failed or only achieved marginal success, he felt bound and determined to make sure this one thrived. Unfortunately, his experience had led him to define a thriving concern as one that planned for only those things you could touch and hold in the present.

Leaping from A to Z

The other founding partner, I'll call him Jesse, couldn't have been more different. A born leader, he almost always inhabited the future. He loved to talk about his grand designs and visions for the company, about how it could diversify into other areas of distribution and even into manufacturing. "I can taste the future," he used to say. In the beginning, his blue-sky vision of the future and Hank's dogmatic focus on the present seemed to complement each other beautifully. However, as the years went by and as the company became established and successful, the difference between the two perspectives became a source of almost constant contention and animosity. Because neither man questioned the company's survival any longer, they had all the more time to strike sparks off each other. Their positions, rather than mellowing, actually grew more and more extreme. Jesse became completely obsessed with the future, and Hank compulsively preoccupied himself with the present. While Jesse busily developed all his long-term strategies and plans for acquiring new business and entering new markets, Hank just as busily planned and budgeted for the day after tomorrow.

Falling from A to Zero

With one partner trudging from A to B and the other soaring from A to Z, the company eventually fell apart. Increasingly irrational toward each other, the two men behaved much like two children fighting over a cake. One wanted to eat it now, the other wanted to save it for tomorrow. Of course, they couldn't have it and eat it too. The power struggle took on such ridiculous proportions that it caused many people in the organization to seek employment elsewhere, and it even caused suppliers to ask serious questions about the ability of these two partners to hold their business together. Over a number of months, this thriving business lost one supplier after another, a turn of events that exacerbated the power struggle and eventually led to bankruptcy. When three or four of the suppliers removed their product lines, it put a financial strain on the company that fueled the raging battle between Hank and Jesse. This all happened surprisingly fast for those of us observing the situation. Unfortunately, the foundation of this company, Hank and Jesse, had been so weakened that when the structure began to crumble, the whole company seemed to self-destruct. As you know, a distribution company depends on suppliers and manufacturers to stay in business, and without them, this business died quickly.

The moral of this story? When someone entrenched in the present comes to blows with someone preoccupied with the future, neither can possibly win. If you view the present and the future as a smooth continuum, you should never fall prey to such a schism. After all, going from A to B is just part of going from A to Z. If you prefer the present perspective of the manager, try to develop an appreciation for thinking that extends further into the future, perhaps not as far as Z, but at least as far as M. If you more comfortably adopt the future viewpoint of the leader, gain an appreciation for those who can make sure you fill in most of the M's, N's, O's, and P's that must occur between A and Z. Whatever you do, don't underestimate the potential for catastrophic conflict over these two orientations.

48

Short Term
plus
Long Term

Managers Concentrate on Short-Term Results;
Leaders Seek Long-Term Results

Managers tend to focus on *short-term*, immediate results, viewing
such results as the only true or viable measure of whether or not
they are doing a good job. To managers, long-term results just don't
seem very real. Leaders, on the other hand, tend to think in terms of
long-term, grand, and often idealistic results. Leaders believe that
focusing on the long term places the short term in perspective. The
mind of the manager argues for the short term as the critical focus
because without it, there will be no long term. Again, it's a matter of
emphasis and sequence.

I once became involved with Laser (a fictitious name), which
was a medium-sized, diversified communications company, whose
president and CEO, vocally heralding the "age of excellence,"
asked me to advise him on developing the skills of insight, sensitivity, focus, versatility, vision and patience I wrote about in an earlier
book, *Creating Excellence*. At least intellectually valuing the long

term, he told me and everyone around him that he wanted to become a much more patient CEO, a trait that would allow his decisions to unfold in the long term. Having concluded that he had focused much too narrowly on short-term results over the past few years, he seemed genuinely intent on promoting a new kind of long-term orientation. As a result, I conducted a session for him and a handful of his top executives. All went well, but in the months that followed I was to detect a distinct discrepancy between the CEO's words and his actions.

Long-Term Words

Laser's CEO, Clyde Brattle (not his real name), thought of himself as every inch a leader, and he talked expansively about future visions and long-range goals. He did so with much persuasiveness and charisma, despite the fact that the company's track record reflected almost exclusive attention to short-range goals. Still, Brattle had become so enamored of the idea of living in the long term that he brought the subject up constantly. "Patience isn't just virtue," he'd proclaim, "it's the future."

After a few months of such ringing words, people within the company began to believe them. Key executives blended their thinking and planning to accommodate five to ten years as well as the traditional two to three-year horizon. New hope and excitement ran through the organization, and as I returned to conduct a follow-up retreat, the morale of the management group seemed to have soared to an all-time high. With the CEO's message having finally gotten across, the management group really had begun developing a combined perspective of short-term and long-term results. While everyone recognized that short-term results mattered in day-to-day operations, they also believed that more long-term results would ensure a prosperous future. To me, as an outsider, the blend appeared to be just right.

Short-Term Actions

Not until the following year did I recontact Laser, and when I did, I got quite a shock. The head of one of Laser's divisions had recently lost his job for failing, as he put it, to deliver on his annual budget. Needless to say, his firing had devastated the rest of the management group, all of whom began to question the CEO's true commitment to building for the long term. From their perspectives, this division head had sacrificed this year's results in order to do just that. When Brattle fired him, that one act demolished months of talk about the future. On my own, I talked with some of the other members of the management group in an effort to understand how one action by the CEO could affect them so deeply. Without exception, each executive wondered out loud whether the CEO really meant what he said about balancing long-term and short-term results or had he simply fallen for a passing fad.

Eventually, I called Brattle to set up an interview to get his side of the story. Before we began, I shared with him some of the feedback I'd heard as well as my own concern that he had "shot himself in the foot" with the firing. In defense of his action, he explained to me that he'd been considering firing that particular division head for some time, and for many reasons, not just because he had not met his annual budget. As we talked at length about the situation and how it had affected the management group, he admitted that often he had taken steps to correct problems or address issues that his management group didn't fully understand and had thus opened himself up to unfounded criticism. "That," he argued, "is what's going on now." At my urging, he decided to air out this whole issue immediately with his management group at a discussion session that I would help facilitate.

Matching Words to Actions

In my experience, few other areas suffer from as much confusion, uncertainty, and miscommunication as the one involving short-term versus long-term results. In this case, when we all got together to discuss the issue, it became quite clear that the management group suspected that the CEO's words masked opposing beliefs. The group did not fully trust Brattle's new commitment to living in the long term, and consequently, when Brattle fired the division head, the group assumed that he had revealed his true preoccupation with the short term. Brattle openly admitted that he had exhibited more of the characteristics of a manager than of a leader and that his past focus on short-term results had certainly created an obstacle to the future. However, he then painstakingly explained the logic behind the termination of the division head and asked his management group to help him find a way to prevent any miscommunication about such actions in the future.

After extensive discussion, it all boiled down to understanding. Only clear, constant, and ongoing understanding among the management group could forestall the sort of confusion and anxiety that so often springs up around the issue of short-term versus long-term results. The group therefore agreed to hold quarterly management sessions designed specifically to review expectations. Over the next year, these sessions led to a deeper understanding all around of the relationship between this year, the following year, and the next five to ten years. In essence, this group concluded that long term comes first, but that it only becomes achievable with concrete short-term steps. While the company should not pursue short-term results at the expense of long-term results, neither should it use the pursuit of long-term results to justify poor performance in the short term. This excuse had provided the "straw" that prompted the CEO to fire the division head, who was simply covering up a string of poor performances.

Both long-term and short-term results are important considerations for any organization. However, it never ceases to amaze me how many businesspeople inordinately focus on one over the other. In balanced and integrated organizations, you can avoid such extremism by consistently stressing, measuring, and rewarding both.

49

Good plus Better

Managers Want Good; Leaders Demand Better

"If it's not broken, don't fix it," says the manager, to which the leader responds, "Fix it even if it's not broken." These words reflect the tendency on the part of managers to feel satisfied when things are going well and on the part of leaders to feel dissatisfied when things aren't getting better. The mind of the manager seems to define progress and performance in terms of poor, fair, good, or excellent or some similar set of categories, and they find anything in the *good* or *excellent* categories eminently acceptable. Of course, the manager at poor or fair wants to get better, just as the manager at good wants to become excellent. However, the categories of progress and performance still come in shades of good or bad. By contrast, the soul of the leader looks at progress and performance not in terms of defined categories of good and bad, but in terms of shades of *better*. In other words, leaders think of progress and performance in terms of a little better, a lot better, or not at all better. Last year I observed both these tendencies in a small business struggling for its identity.

Can Good Be Bad?

I became involved with K-M Technology, a small high-tech company, as an adviser to its chairman and CEO, whom I'll refer to as Dunhill. Dunhill was the sort of leader who strove constantly to make his company better and better and still better. Unfortunately, Dunhill failed to reward people sufficiently for the good things they did, and consequently, K-M Technology experienced a high level of turnover among management and employees alike. While Dunhill accepted the notion intellectually that you build better on a foundation of good, he just couldn't bring himself to recognize good performance because he feared that doing so would make people feel satisfied and never move to get better. In essence, he felt that good is bad, and even though he sometimes did tell his people that they were doing a good job, just as I advised him to do, everyone in the company seemed to sense that he was simply going through the motions.

In reality, Dunhill never felt satisfied, and his managers and people knew it. Always pressured to get better and better, people eventually succumbed to the strain of it all and left for less stressful pastures. Some called it "burnout," but I called it the "better can be bad" syndrome. One example of this occurred when K-M Technology's chief engineer came up with a product innovation that propelled the company well ahead of its competition. This innovation, which made possible extremely accurate sensing instruments for use in space, helped K-M Technology increase by a factor of two the accuracy of its equipment. Dunhill lauded this wonderful breakthrough to the press but treated it like "business as usual" with the chief engineer and his staff.

Can Better Be Bad?

I felt strongly in this case that the quest for getting better was compromising K-M Technology's long-term development. Dunhill would never rest and never enjoy the fruits of his labor or the accomplishments of his organization, and he would never let up his relentless push, push, push ahead. Ultimately, turnover took a heavy toll, and all the pushing in the world couldn't make things better. The chief engineer left in a huff and took with him an alarming number of loyal subordinates. Dunhill couldn't find his match anywhere in the industry, at least at first.

During some intimate and personal discussions, I argued heatedly with Dunhill that better can sometimes be bad, but my words fell on deaf ears. "I'm too old to change," he insisted. "If you don't," I replied, "I don't think you'll ever build this company beyond its current size." When he didn't believe me, I told him I had done everything I could for his company and concluded our relationship.

Better Is Always Better

Well, it turned out that I was dead wrong in my assessment of K-M Technology, a fact that became painfully clear as the company doubled in size again and again in the following years. Dunhill proved to me that better can always be better. The turnover rate actually declined as he amazingly attracted more and more people like himself who would never settle for good, but who would always strive for better. At the time of my involvement with the organization, Dunhill had not yet learned how to find and attract like-minded leaders. Now he had. In a recent conversation, he admitted to me that my advice had not been completely wasted because it had deepened his resolve to find a way to prove me and the notion that "better is sometimes bad" wrong. And, obviously, he had.

Of course, not all organizations can operate the way Dunhill's did. Some employ more managers who can live happily with the good. If, however, you have more leaders than managers in your organization, you can stress better and better. The biggest problems arise when you try to forge some combination of the two. While this small business struggled most when it employed similar numbers of managers and leaders, it succeeded when it had weeded out most of the managers. In reality, it had become a leadership-driven organization. This may explain, at least partially, why good organizations have such a hard time becoming better ones. Based on my experience with this company and many others, I believe that if you want to perpetuate good, you should rely on managers, but if you want to perpetuate better, you should look to leaders. Since, in reality, organizations go through some periods when they want to perpetuate good and others when they want to perpetuate better, the balanced and integrated ones learn to blend the ebb and flow of the manager/leader mix. They don't vacillate between one and the other, nor do they place the two orientations at adversarial odds. They keep the tension between good and better in all their communications. By doing so, they increase the appreciation of managers for leaders, and vice versa. This then becomes the germination point for the real blending of the two.

Conclusion

How You Can Begin Tapping the Natural Tension Between Managers and Leaders

Empowered Management/Leadership Environments

Exceptional organizations achieve greatness by focusing their strategies, unifying their cultures, aligning their strategies and cultures to exploit change, and empowering their people toward enduring effectiveness and results. When they succeed in doing so, they benefit from satisfied customers, fulfilled employees, capable management teams, rewarded shareholders, contented communities, and exceptional bottom-line results. While many organizations can develop strategic focus, cultural unity, dynamic adaptation to change, maximum individual effectiveness, and spectacular results for a brief period of time, it takes an empowered management/leadership environment to perpetuate these capabilities far into the future. Such an environment taps the natural tension between managers and leaders, bringing about a binding together of all the major candidly. I believe we'll need such balanced and integrated environments to guide our organizations profitably and prudently into the next century.

To create such empowered environments and organizations, managers and leaders need not betray or ignore their unique talents and abilities, but they must learn to orchestrate every different perspective and orientation along the management/leadership continuum into a harmonious symphony. Even an entrenched manager or leader can achieve a more balanced and integrated organization, provided he or she takes the time to value and deploy a diverse range of management/leadership skills.

Creating An Empowered Management/Leadership Environment

I define an empowered management/leadership environment as a "climate that taps the natural tension between managers and leaders and thereby achieves an enduring level of willingness and ability among people to achieve outstanding results." Such empowerment results from:

- Accurate Self-awareness
- Understanding Different Perspectives
- Valuing Attitudes
- Candid Communications
- Common Purposes

The more completely people realize these five traits, the more empowered they and their organizations become and the more enduring grow their levels of willingness and ability. But how, specifically, can you develop these traits?

- *Accurate Self-awareness*: Only when you accurately understand yourself and your strengths and limitations can you begin to appreciate the different perspectives of others. Using Appendix A, assess your own orientations, perspectives, and preferences.
- *Understanding Different Perspectives*: Once you have assessed yourself, you can evaluate your perspectives, as well as those of

assess your own orientations, perspectives, and preferences, as well as those of your team and organization.

- *Understanding Different Perspectives*: Once you have assessed yourself, you can evaluate your limitations, as well as those of your management team and organization using Appendix B.
- *Valuing Attitudes*: Given a clearer understanding of your own perspectives and how they might differ from others, you should weigh whether you truly appreciate and value different orientations. Using Appendix D, evaluate your own (your team's and your organization's) willingness and ability to value differing perspectives in your current management/leadership environments. Remember, people working in empowered environments always exhibit a "valuing attitude" that allows different orientations, perspectives, and talents to blend together for the benefit of all.
- *Candid Communications*: In order to take full advantage of the differences among people in an organization, you will need to develop an open and honest communications process, one that helps people understand others as they would wish to be understood themselves. You can begin to initiate such a process by using the data gleaned from Appendices A through D as a basis for ongoing discussion.
- *Common Purposes*: Accurate self-awareness, balanced perspectives, valuing attitudes, and candid communications represent crucial aspects of an empowered management/leadership environment, but they can accomplish little if they lack clear purpose and direction. Appendix E will help you match your current orientations with those needed in the future. Working through this exercise can help you determine necessary future development and select the appropriate empowering purpose.

With each element in place, empowered management/leadership environments can provide "fertile soil" for the growth of truly great organizations. By tapping the natural tension between managers and leaders, an organization can plant the seed and provide the ongoing nutrition for an era of unparalleled results by any and every measure of success.

Appendices

A word of caution: Since the following assessments represent "shorthand" adaptations of sophisticated tools for assessing and developing an empowered management/leadership environment, you should avoid relying too heavily on the results you obtain with them. Even though they cannot replace a full and detailed assessment, they should provide useful clues for improving your current situation.

Management Perspectives Group's full methodology combines personal interviewing and observation with any number of surveys and tests — MBTI (Myers-Briggs Type Indicator), DISC (Dominant, Influencing, Steady, Compliant), FIRO-B (Fundamental Interpersonal Relationship Orientation-Behavior), Thomas-Kilman Conflict Mode Instrument, MPGA (Management Perspectives Group Assessments), etc. — and a great deal of analysis based on experience. You may want to augment the following exercises with some outside consulting.

Appendix A: Self Assessment

Directions: The following questionnaire does in a brief, encapsulated way what a skilled facilitator or consultant might do to help people in organizations get a firmer grip on their preferences and perceptions. Because the questionnaire deals with preferences as opposed to abilities, and initial perceptions rather than total perceptions, note that although you may actually use both choices, one probably describes you better or more accurately than the other. (Remember, you're not measuring your ability, only your preferences and initial perceptions.) With that in mind, circle the number or letter that appeals to you most or describes you best.

Practical		*Conceptual*	
You prefer practicality.	1	You prefer ingenuity.	A
You enjoy books that state their message literally and simply, and hit the point.	1	You enjoy books that stimulate your imagination through unusual or thought-provoking language.	A
You prefer being realistic.	1	You prefer being imaginative.	A
You are sensible.	1	You are original.	A
You are a person who is down-to-earth, focused on the present.	1	You are a person who is visionary, focused on the future.	A
You think of yourself as being pragmatic and factual.	1	You think of yourself as being innovative and philosophical.	A
You prefer to live in a world of facts.	1	You prefer to live in a world of theories and ideas.	A
You prefer the known.	1	You prefer the unknown.	A
You prefer to build something.	1	You prefer to invent something.	A
You rely on common sense.	1	You rely on vision.	A
Others describe you as conventional.	1	Others describe you as unpredictable.	A

Write the number of 1's and A's circled.   __   __

Reasonable

In dealing with others, you use reasonableness and consistency of thought.	2
You use logic over empathy.	2
You are firm.	2
You make decisions based on thinking.	2
You are analytical.	2
You make judgments with your head.	2
Your temperament would be described as hard.	2
You are decisive.	2
You are firm-minded.	2
In deciding something important, you do the logical thing, no matter how you feel about it.	2
You prefer examining situations.	2

Write the number of 2's and B's circled.   ___

Empathetic

In dealing with others, you use feelings and harmony of emotions.	B
You use empathy over logic.	B
You are gentle.	B
You make decisions based on feeling.	B
You are sympathetic.	B
You make decisions with your heart.	B
Your temperament would be described as soft.	B
You are impulsive.	B
You are warm-hearted.	B
In deciding something important, you trust your feelings about what is best to do.	B
You prefer relating to others.	B

___

Decisive

You are the orderly type.	3
You prefer to plan ahead.	3
You prefer the systematic.	3
You are methodical.	3
You think life should consist of specific standards.	3
You are uncomfortable until things are done.	3
You prefer a lifestyle of putting things in their proper place.	3
You prefer making things happen.	3
You are more decisive than curious.	3
You have long-lasting friendships.	3
You have settled opinions.	3

Write the number of 3's and C's circled.   ___

Flexible

You are the relaxed type.	C
You prefer to be spontaneous.	C
You prefer the casual.	C
You are easy-going.	C
You believe we should "live and let live" within reason.	C
You do not feel an urgency to get things done right away.	C
You prefer a lifestyle of letting things fall where they will.	C
You prefer letting things happen.	C
You are more curious than decisive.	C
You take on friendships easily; may also neglect, drop, and pick them up again.	C
Your opinions are still settling.	C

___

Rating Yourself: Determine which of the 1's or A's; 2's or B's; and 3's or C's totalled the highest, then list the three highest to find your composite rating. For example, if you circled *seven 1's* and four A's; three 2's and *eight B's*; *six 3's* and five C's, then your rating would be *1B3*. Identify your own rating below:

More 1's or A's? More 2's or B's? More 3's or C's?

_____ _____ _____

Once you have identified the composite rating that best describes your preferences, place yourself on the following Management-Leadership Continuum. Next, consult the shorthand description matrices for each category.

Management-Leadership Continuum

Management | | | | | | | Leadership
Oriented   123 12C 1B3 A23 1BC A2C AB3 ABC   Oriented

Composite Ratings

Composite Ratings

123	Practical, Reasonable, and Decisive
12C	Practical, Reasonable, and Flexible
1B3	Practical, Empathetic, and Decisive
A23	Conceptual, Reasonable, and Decisive
1BC	Practical, Empathetic, and Flexible
A2C	Conceptual, Reasonable, and Flexible
AB3	Conceptual, Empathetic, and Decisive
ABC	Conceptual, Empathetic, and Flexible

Shorthand Description of 1's and A's
(based on chapters from the book)

	If you identified yourself as a "1", you prefer or perceive first:	*If you identified yourself as an "A", you prefer or perceive first:*
Competitive Strategy/Advantage	Danger Version Incremental	Opportunity Vision Sweeping
Organizational Culture/Capability	Instruction Control	Inspiration Empower
External/Internal Change	Duplicate Reaction Reorganize Refine	Originate Proaction Rethink Revolutionize
Individual Effectiveness/Style	Logical Thinking Skepticism Duties	Lateral Thinking Optimism Dreams
Bottom Line Performance/Results	Present Short-Term Good	Future Long-Term Better

Comments: Write down which of the "1" or "A" orientations you think accurately describe your preference or initial perception and which do not. Keep in mind that when people are under pressure or stress, they often exhibit the opposite orientation from their preferred orientation.

Shorthand Description of 2's and B's
(based on chapters from the book)

	If you identified yourself as a "2", you prefer or perceive first:	If you identified yourself as a "B", you prefer or perceive first:
Competitive Strategy/Advantage	Strategy Markets Weaknesses	Culture Customers Strengths
Organizational Culture/Capability	Authority Programs Policy Consistency	Influence People Example Commitment
External/Internal Change	Fasten Complexity	Unfasten Simplicity
Individual Effectiveness/Style	Methods Hierarchy Science	Motives Equality Art
Bottom Line Performance/Results	Compensation Tangible	Satisfaction Intangible

Comments: Write down which of the "2" or "B" orientations you think accurately describe your preference or initial perception and which do not. Keep in mind that when people are under pressure or stress, they often exhibit the opposite orientation from their preferred orientation.

Shorthand Description of 3's and C's
(based on chapters from the book)

	If you identified yourself as a "3", you prefer or perceive first:	If you identified yourself as a "C", you prefer or perceive first:
Competitive Strategy/Advantage	Isolate Solutions Rivals	Integrate Problems Partners
Organizational Culture/Capability	Uniformity MBO Releasing	Unity MWBA Keeping
External/Internal Change	Stability Compromise Plans	Crisis Polarize Experiments
Individual Effectiveness/Style	Smoothing Taking Charge Formality	Confronting Letting Go Informality
Bottom Line Performance/Results	Performance Dependence Conserving	Potential Independence Risking

Comments: Write down which of the "3" or "C" orientations you think accurately describe your preference or initial perception and which do not. Keep in mind that when people are under pressure or stress, they often exhibit the opposite orientation from their preferred orientation.

Appendix B: Team Assessment

Directions: After collecting self-assessments from each member of your team, place each person along the following Team Management-Leadership Continuum.

Team Management-Leadership Continuum

Management
Oriented

| | | | | | | | |

123 12C 1B3 A23 1BC A2C AB3 ABC

Leadership
Oriented

Composite Ratings

Comments: Is your team balanced? Do you see any patterns?

Appendix C: Organization Assessment

Directions: Complete the following questionnaire to assess your organization. Ignore the parenthetical codes for the time being.

	Accurate	Somewhat Accurate	Somewhat Inaccurate	Inaccurate
1. Your organization pursues strategies that do not change the basic nature and definition of its business in the marketplace. (MD1)	4	3	2	1
2. Your organization constantly formulates strategies that create the right kind of environment for innovation to flourish. (LD1)	4	3	2	1
3. Your organization attempts to pursue both same-game (mirroring the marketplace) and new-game (innovative) strategies. (CO1)	4	3	2	1
4. Your organization pursues nothing but strategies that react to the market. (VP1)	4	3	2	1
5. Your organization's strategies take into account the fluid nature of the marketplace, the industry, the competition, suppliers, customers, society and the world. (BI1)	4	3	2	1
6. Your organization's strategies look like those of its competitors. (MD2)	4	3	2	1
7. Your organization creates a new sub-culture for each new product line or extension. (LD2)	4	3	2	1

		Accurate	Somewhat Accurate	Somewhat Inaccurate	Inaccurate
8.	Your organization tries to insulate a new product area from more mature areas of business, encouraging competition between the new and the more mature product areas. (CO1)	4	3	2	1
9.	Your organization's culture vacillates as strategies change according to market activities. (VP2)	4	3	2	1
10.	Your organization steadily renews its culture to take full advantage of changing circumstances in the marketplace and to prepare its people with the capabilities they need to respond appropriately to change. (BI2)	4	3	2	1
11.	Your organization strives to perpetuate the culture that it has been developing throughout its history. (MD3)	4	3	2	1
12.	Your organization relishes crisis and chaos that often attend big changes in the marketplace. (LD3)	4	3	2	1
13.	Your organization keeps trying to change its culture. (CO3)	4	3	2	1
14.	Your organization's approaches and processes move from structured to unstructured and back again in reaction to circumstances. (VP3)	4	3	2	1
15.	Your organization blends its need for both stability and crisis in a way that makes change easy for its people to anticipate and handle. (BI3)	4	3	2	1

	Accurate	Somewhat Accurate	Somewhat Inaccurate	Inaccurate
16. Your organization tries to absorb external and internal change quickly in order to avoid disrupting the organization's stability. (MD4)	4	3	2	1
17. Your organization's teams operate according to unstructured approaches and processes. (LD4)	4	3	2	1
18. Your organization desires stability and crisis simultaneously, using crisis to disrupt stability and stability to interrupt crisis. (CO4)	4	3	2	1
19. Managers within your organization want to remove the leaders from power and *vice versa*. (VP4)	4	3	2	1
20. Your organization remains dynamic in its approaches and processes, modifying them when necessary, but never tossing aside existing standards without good reason. (BI4)	4	3	2	1
21. So many goals, objectives, policies, and standards exist within your organization, that when change does occur, people know exactly how to factor it into the system. (MD5)	4	3	2	1
22. Your organization emphasizes intangible, long-term results. (LD5)	4	3	2	1
23. Your organization prides itself on maintaining an equal emphasis on structured and unstructured approaches and processes. (CO5)	4	3	2	1

	Accurate	Somewhat Accurate	Somewhat Inaccurate	Inaccurate
24. A warring attitude dominates relationships between leaders and managers in your organization. (VP5)	4	3	2	1
25. Your organiztion combines tangible with intangible and short-term with long-term results so that its people cannot talk about one without talking about the other. (BI5)	4	3	2	1
26. Your organization loves structured approaches and processes because it believes that they will provide the kind of stable effectiveness the organization seeks. (MD6)	4	3	2	1
27. Your organization suffers from doubt, uncertainty, lack of identity, and clear direction because it shifts wildly between leadership and management. (VP6)	4	3	2	1
28. Your organization deeply values differing perspectives and orientations, is committed to openness and candor in all communications and interactions, and has an aggressive willingness to face up to realities and issues. (BI6)	4	3	2	1
29. Your organization expects nothing but tangible, short-term results. (MD7)	4	3	2	1

Rating Your Organization:

Management/Leadership Environment	Total the scores for these questions:	Divide the total by this number:	Write the result here:
Management-Driven (MD)	1,6,11,16,21,26,29	7	_____
Leadership-Driven (LD)	2,7,12,17,22	5	_____
Conflict-Oriented (CO)	3,8,13,18,23	5	_____
Vacillation-Prone (VP)	4,9,14,19,24,27	6	_____
Balanced-Integrated (BI)	5,10,15,20,25,28	6	_____

Plot the average score for each management/leadership environment (the far right column above) on this graph. The completed graph will display the organization's preferred or existing management/leadership environment.

	0	1	2	3	4
Management-Driven*	├───────┼───────┼───────┼───────┤
Leadership-Driven*	├───────┼───────┼───────┼───────┤
Conflict-Oriented*	├───────┼───────┼───────┼───────┤
Vacillation-Prone*	├───────┼───────┼───────┼───────┤
Balanced-Integrated*	├───────┼───────┼───────┼───────┤

*See the charts in the Introduction to review orientations of the different management/leadership environments toward strategy, culture, change, effectiveness, and results.

Comments: How balanced is your organization?

Appendix D: Valuing Attitudes Assessment

Directions: On the following page, indicate the levels of willingness and ability to value differing perspectives that exist in your management/leadership environment(s). Letters express willingness, numbers express ability. Descriptions of willingness (attitude) are labeled A, B, C, and D. Descriptions of ability (understanding) are labeled 1, 2, 3, and 4. Once you have made the individual assessments of willingness and ability, combine them to obtain the value rating (for example, a "B" willingness rating and a "3" ability rating give you a "B3" value rating).

Willingness (Attitude)

D   They have to see it my way.

C   Sooner or later, they will see it my way.

B   If I am to be understood, I must first seek to understand.

A   If I were one of them, I would very possibly do things the same way they do.

Ability (Understanding)

4   Everyone is basically the same; differences can be explained by age, sex, or education.

3   Everyone is different, with distinct needs, values, and interests.

2   Differences among people can be clearly articulated, either verbally or in writing.

1   The distinct needs, values, and interests of different people can be acted upon.

	Willingness (Attitude)		Ability (Understanding)		Value Rating
Self	D C B A	+	4 3 2 1	=	_____
Team	D C B A	+	4 3 2 1	=	_____
Organ.	D C B A	+	4 3 2 1	=	_____

Now locate your position, by value rating, on the following chart. Then, consider an action plan to achieve or maintain the desired valuing levels by referring to the shorthand strategies section.

Valuing Characteristics
Willingness To Value

Strong   Weak

	1	2	3	4

Ability To Value

Clear A, B	*Description:* Empowered Valuing *Characteristics:* Strong attitude/willingness to value. Clear understanding/ability to value.	*Description:* Unmotivated Valuing *Characteristics:* Weak attitude/willingness to value. Clear understanding/ability to value.
Unclear C, D	*Description:* Undirected Valuing *Characteristics:* Strong attitude/willingness to value. Unclear understanding/ability to value.	*Description:* Under Valuing *Characteristics:* Weak attitude/willingness to value. Unclear understanding/ability to value.

Shorthand Strategies for Increasing Valuing Levels

Empowered Valuing	Unmotivated Valuing
Ask: How are we doing?	**Ask:** What's in it for us?
Situation: Although strong attitudes and clear understandings exist, participants need to know how they are doing on a regular basis. Resource and peer support might be needed from time to time.	**Situation:** The combination of clear understanding with weak attitudes can create the most frustrating of all situations. Although very able, the participants are not willing to value without "win" solutions.
Strategy: Obtain appropriate support, regular feedback, and encouragement.	**Strategy:** Develop motivation tracks that are personal, timely, and clear.
Undirected Valuing	**Under Valuing**
Ask: Where are we going?	**Ask:** Why are we here?
Situation: Strong attitudes with understandings that are not clear can lead to "feel good" environments that accomplish little. People cannot value what they know nothing about.	**Situation:** Weak attitudes and unclear understandings make valuing in a management/leadership environment almost impossible.
Strategy: Schedule educational, training, and awareness sessions.	**Strategy:** Address the needs of understanding first, then tackle the concerns of attitude.

Appendix E: Future Assessment

Directions: In light of the foregoing assessments and your organization's future concerns, requirements, and issues relating to competitive strategy/advantage, organizational culture/capability, external/
internal change, individual effectiveness/style, and bottom-line per-
formance/results, what modifications, changes, reinforcements, or
new directions would you recommend?

For Yourself:

For Your Team:

For Your Organization:

Bibliography

Bennett, James E., and McKinsey & Company. "Planning Strategically: The Key to Corporate Survival and Success." Business Week's Strategic Planning Conference, Toronto, November 10, 1980.

Bennis, Warren and Burt Nanus. *Leaders*. New York: Harper & Row, 1985.

Bennis, Warren. *On Becoming A Leader*. Reading, Mass: Addison-Wesley, 1989.

Burns, James MacGregor. *Leadership*. New York: Harper & Row, 1978.

Drucker, Peter F. "Management and the World's Work." *Harvard Business Review*, September–October 1988.

Drucker, Peter F. *The New Realities*. New York: Harper & Row, 1989.

Dumaine, Brian. "Those Highflying PepsiCo Managers." *Fortune*, April 10, 1989.

Ferguson, Charles H. "From the People Who Brought You Voodoo Economics." *Harvard Business Review*, May–June 1988.

Gilder, George. "The Revitalization of Everything: The Law of the Microcosm. *Harvard Business Review*, March–April, 1988.

Hickman, Craig R., and Michael A. Silva. *Creating Excellence*. New York: New American Library, 1984.

Kiechel, Walter, III. "The Case Against Leaders." *Fortune*, November 21, 1988.

Kotter, John. *The Leadership Factor*. New York: The Free Press, 1988.

Levitt, Ted. "On Agility and Stability" (From the Editor). *Harvard Business Review*, March–April 1988.

Levitt, Ted. "Command and Consent" (From the Editor). *Harvard Business Review*, July–August 1988.

Levitt, Ted. "Making Sense" (From the Editor). *Harvard Business Review*, September–October, 1989.

McGregor, Douglas. *The Human Side of Enterprise*. New York: McGraw-Hill, 1960.

McKinsey & Company. "Building a More Effective Commercial Banking System — Without Financial Chaos." McKinsey & Company White Paper, June 10, 1981, Revised August 17, 1981.

Odiorne, George S. *Management By Objectives*. New York: Pitman Publishing Co., 1965.

Ohmae, Kenichi. *The Mind of the Strategist*. New York: McGraw-Hill, 1982.

Pascale, Richard Tanner, and Anthony G. Athos. *The Art of Japanese Management*. New York: Simon & Schuster, 1981.

Peters, Tom. *Thriving on Chaos*. New York: Alfred A. Knopf, 1988.

Tichy, Noel M., and Mary Anne Devanna. *The Transformational Leader*. New York: John Wiley & Sons, 1986.

Zaleznik, Abraham. "Managers and Leaders: Are They Different?" *Harvard Business Review*, May–June 1977.

Zaleznik, Abraham. *The Managerial Mystique*. New York: Harper & Row, 1989.

Index

Akers, John, 7
Apple Computer, 7, 14
Artistic approach to management and
     leadership, 216–219
Assessment
  future, 281
  organization, 272–276
  self, 265–270
  team, 271
  valuing attitudes, 277–280
Assets, conservation and risk of, 240–243
Attitudes, valuing, 263
Authority, of managers, 99–102

Bain & Company, 204
Balanced and integrated environments, 20,
     45–51
  benefiting from, 51
  characteristics of, 45–48
  leaders in, 48–49
  managers in, 48–49
  strengths of, 49–50
  weaknesses of, 50
Balanced perspectives, 263
Bennis, Warren, 15, 16, 282
Booz, Allen, 204
Boston Consulting Group, 204
Bottom-line performance results. *See*
     Performance results
Burnout, 258
Burns, James MacGregor, 15, 282
Business Week, 16

Calloway, Wayne, 5
"Case Against Leaders, The" (Kiechel), 16
Change, 139–181
  balanced and integrated environment and,
     20, 46–47, 49
  complexity and, 160–164
  compromise and, 155–159
  conflict-oriented environment and, 20, 36
  crisis and, 141–144
  duplication and, 145–149
  experimentation and, 169–173
  fastening/unfastening and, 150–154
  leadership-driven environment and, 20, 30,
     32, 33–34
  leaders vs. managers and, 11
  management-dominated environment and,
     20, 24, 26–27
  originality and, 145–149
  planning and, 169–173
  polarization and, 155–159
  proaction and, 165–168
  refining and, 178–181
  reorganization and, 174–177
  rethinking and, 174–177

revolutionizing and, 178–181
simplicity and, 160–164
stability and, 141–144
vacillation-prone environment and, 20, 41
Changing-game strategies, 45–46, 59, 54
Claiborne, Elisabeth, 14
Commitment, 135–138
Communication, 192–193, 263
Compensation, 236–239
Competition, 83–86
  new style, 84–85
  old style, 84
Competitive strategy/advantage, 53–95
  balanced and integrated environment and,
     20, 45–46, 49
  conflict-oriented environment and, 20, 35–36
  correlating and, 70–74
  culture and, 55–60
  customers and, 79–82
  isolating and, 70–74
  leadership-driven environment and, 20, 30
  leaders vs. managers and, 1–6, 8
  management-dominated environment and,
     20, 23, 25
  markets and, 79–82
  opportunities and, 61–64
  partners and, 83–86
  problems and, 75–78
  rivals and, 83–86
  solutions and, 75–78
  strategic strengths and weaknesses and, 91–95
  vacillation-prone environment and, 20, 40–41
  versions and, 65–69
  vision and, 65–69
Complexity, 160–164
Compromise, 155–159
Conflict culture, 36
Conflict-oriented environments, 20, 35–39
  benefiting from, 39
  characteristics of, 35–37
  leaders in, 37
  managers in, 37
  strengths of, 38
  weaknesses of, 38
Conflict, smoothing and confronting, 204–207
Confrontation, 204–207
Conservation of assets, 240–243
Consistency, 135–138
Continuums, manager-leader, 8, 9, 11, 12, 267,
     271
Control, and managers, 9, 127–130
Correlating, 70–74
Creating Excellence (Hickman), 253, 282
Crisis
  opportunity and, 61
  stability and, 141–144
Criticism, 199–203

For More Information

If you would like to receive additional assessment materials
and other information on management/leadership
environments, call:

Management Perspectives Group
1-800-537-3065